John Neely

The Confederate States Speller and Reader

John Neely

The Confederate States Speller and Reader

ISBN/EAN: 9783337812652

Printed in Europe, USA, Canada, Australia, Japan

Cover: Foto ©Thomas Meinert / pixelio.de

More available books at **www.hansebooks.com**

THE

CONFEDERATE STATES

SPELLER & READER:

CONTAINING THE

PRINCIPLES and PRACTICE of ENGLISH ORTHOGRAPHY and ORTHÖEPY

SYSTEMATICALLY DEVELOPED.

Designed to Accord with the "Present Usage of Literary and Well-Bred Society."

IN THREE PARTS.

FOR THE USE OF SCHOOLS AND FAMILIES.

By Rev JOHN NEELY.

PUBLISHED BY A. BLEAKLEY, AUGUSTA, GA.
1864.

PUBLISHER'S ADVERTISEMENT.

The book here offered to Southern Teachers, is neither a reprint, nor a medley hurriedly got up. It is an original book, as far as such a book can be original; and has been prepared with the utmost care, by a practical teacher, whose experience of more than forty years in his profession has enabled him to judge what are the wants both of preceptor and of pupil. A large portion of the manuscript was written several years ago; and the "Speller and Reader" is not now published merely to fill up a gap for a time, and to be thrown aside when other books of its class can be procured from our former literary emporium. It claims at least equality with the very best of these productions; and it is intended to hold its position *permanently* in the face of all such competitors; nor do we entertain any doubt that it will be found, on trial, worthy to take the stand which it assumes in its title page, that of the "Confederate States Speller and Reader." In the simplicity of its development of principles, and in the ease with which it conducts the learner from step to step in his progress, it will be found to differ widely from its predecessors both Northern and

Southern. The Geographical and Scriptural names have received the most minute attention. They are all carefully accented, and whenever necessary their pronunciation marked in Italics; and teachers will doubtless be thankful for this assistance in their labors. In fine, nothing has been neglected, which might render this a useful book, not merely in the initiatory, but in the more advanced stages of education. If the maxim on its first page is faithfully carried out, we believe we hazard little in saying that this little manual cannot fail to prove itself to be all that it pretends to be; and that the teacher who has once used it will rest satisfied that in this respect at least, his wants are well and fully supplied.

We trust, therefore, that a speedy sale of this first edition will afford us an opportunity of issuing another, with such improvements as shall leave nothing to desire.

CONFEDERATE STATES
SPELLER AND READER.

ALPHABET.

A	B	C	D
E	F	G	H
I	J	K	L
M	N	O	P
Q	R	S	T
U	V	W	X
Y	Z	&	Œ

SMALL ALPHABET.

a b c d e f

g h i j k l

m n o p q

r s t u v w

x y z & æ

NUMERALS.

1 2 3 4 5 6 7 8 9 10 11 12
13 14 15 16 17 18 19 20

ROMAN LETTERS.

A B C D E F G H I J K L M
N O P Q R S T U V W X Y Z &
a b c d e f g h i j k l m n o p
q r s t u v w x y z

ITALICS.

A B C D E F G H I J K L M N O
P Q R S T U V W X Y Z &

a b c d e f g h i j k l m n o p q r s t u
v w x y z

EXERCISES ON THE ALPHABET.

n c l k h f s p d z y j

p w v m b i r u t a e

r g u o l q w f s d c x

Comma (,) Semi-Colon (;) Colon (:) Period (.)
Hyphen (-) Apostrophe (') Interrogation (?)
Exclamation (!)

VOWELS, a e i o u, and w and y when they
do not begin a syllable. The other letters are
CONSONANTS.

Maxim to be Observed in Using this Book:

LET EVERY SPELLING LESSON BE MADE A
READING LESSON;
EVERY READING LESSON A SPELLING LESSON.

1. *Spell each Lesson on the Book.* 2. *Read it downward in
columns.* 3. *Read it across.* 4. *Spell it off the Book.*
5. *Name any Syllable pointed to.* 6. *Point out any
Syllable named.*

The sounds of the vowels are unmarked for want of
suitable type.

The soft sound of *c* (like s), as in *city*, is marked by an
italic letter.

The hard sound (like *k*) is unmarked.

The soft sound of *g* (like *j*), as in *gem*, is marked by an
italic letter.

The hard sound, as in *gun*, is unmarked.

The soft sound of *ch* (like *tsh*), as in *church*, is marked
by italic letters.

The hard sound (like *k*) is unmarked.

The flat sound of *th*, as in *this*, is marked by italic letters.

The sharp sound, as in *think*, is unmarked.

PART I.

ELEMENTARY PRINCIPLES.

SYLLABLES AND WORDS OF ONE AND OF TWO LETTERS.

No. 1—I. *Syllables. Vowel Long.*

C before E, I and Y, soft like S.   G before E, I and Y,
soft like J.

ba	be bee	bi	bo	bu	by
ca	ce	ci	co	cu	cy
da	de	di	do	du	dy
fa	fe fee	fi	fo	fu	fy
ga	ge	gi	go	gu	gy
ha	he	hi	ho	hu	hy

No. 2—II.   *Syllables.   Vowel Long.*

ja	je	ji	jo	ju	jy
ka	ke	ki	ko	ku	ky
la	le lee	li	lo	lu	ly
ma	me	mi	mo	mu	my
na	ne	ni	no	nu	ny
pa	pe	pi	po	pu	py

No. 3—III.   *Syllables.   Vowel Long.*

ra	re	ri	ro	ru	ry
sa	se see	si	so	su	sy
ta	te	ti	to	tu	ty
va	ve	vi	vo	vu	vy
wa	we	wi	wo		wy
ya	ye	yi	yo	yu	
za	ze	zi	zo	zu	zy

No. 4—IV   *Words taken from the Syllables in the preceding Nos.   Vowel long.*

be	bee	oh (o)	no
he	fee	go	so
me	lee	ho	wo
we	see	jo	by
ye	I	lo	fy

Exceptions differing in sound of Vowel.

a (ah)	la (law)	ha (hah)
ma (mah)	pa (pah)	do (doo)

No. 5—V

I go.	Ye do.	To me.	Wo to me!
Go I?	Do we?	Be ye.	Do we go?
We go.	O ye.	Ye go.	No: ye go.
Go we?	By me.	My pa.	Ho! my ma!
I do.	O ma!	I do so.	I go by

No. 6—VI.

Do I go so?	Do ye so to me?
Ha! do ye so?	La! my pa! he by me!
Ye go by me.	Ho! to me ye do so.
Lo! I go by	To pa: to ma: to me.
Do so to me.	Ha! go ye so by pa?
Do we go so?	La! I go to ma.
O pa! we go.	No: we go by to pa.
So do I go.	My pa! be by me.

No. 7—VII. Syllables. Vowel Short.

ab	eb ebb	ib	ob	ub
ac	ec	ic	oc	uc
ad add	ed	id	od	ud
af	ef	if	of off	uf
ag	eg egg	ig	og	ug
aj	ej	ij	oj	uj

No. 8—VIII. Syllables. Vowel Short.

ak	ek	ik	ok	uk
al	el ell	il ill	ol	ul
am	em	im	om	um
an ann	en	in inn	on	un
ap	ep	ip	op	up
ar	er err	ir	or	ur

No. 9—IX. Syllables. Vowel Short.

as ass	es	is	os	us
at	et	it	ot	ut
av	ev	iv	ov	uv
ax	ex	ix	ox	ux
az	ez	iz	oz	uz

No. 10—X. *Words taken from the Syllables in the three preceding Nos.*

am	in	or	ann	err
an	is	ox	ass	ill
as	it	up	ebb	inn
at	of (ov)	us	egg	odd
if	on	add	ell	off

I am up.   Is pa up?   Ma is up.   I or he.
Is he up?   Do go on.   So am I.   Lo! an ox.

No. 11—XI.

Go up to it.
Is he at it?
It is on me.
Wo to us!
Do as I do.
Oh fy! go up.
Ma! do go by.
La! I am on.
Ann is ill.
If so, it is odd.
He is off on an ass.
An ass or an ox?

He is at an inn.
Do we err?
Is it an egg?
Add it up.
See if it is a bee.
As ma is up, so am I.
Oh! an ox is at it.
Ha! he is up to us.
If I am on it, so is he.
He or I am up on it.
He is to go on it so.
Am I to go on it? So is pa.

No. 12—XII. *Words of three Letters. Vowel Short.*

-ab	-ib	fob	cub	-ic	pad
cab	bib	hob	dub	tic	sad
dab	fib	job	hub	-ad	wad
mab	nib	mob	rub	bad	-ed
nab	rib	nob	tub	gad	bed
tab	-ob	rob	-ac	had	fed
-eb	bob	sob	lac	lad	led
web	cob	-ub	sac	mad	red

No. 13—XIII. Words of three Letters. Vowel Short

-id	-od	-ud	hag	beg	gig
bid	cod	bud	jag	keg	jig
did	hod	cud	lag	leg	pig
hid	nod	mud	nag	peg	rig
kid	pod	-ag	rag	-ig	wig
lid	rod	bag	tag	big	-og
mid	sod	fag	wag	dig	bog
rid	tod	gag	-eg	fig	cog

No. 14—XIV Words of three Letters. Vowel Short

dog	hug	dam	-im	sum	ran
fog	jug	ham	dim	-an	tan
hog	lug	jam	him	ban	van
jog	mug	ram	rim	can	wan
log	pug	sam	-um	dan	-en
-ug	rug	-em	gum	fan	den
bug	tug	gem	hum	man	fen
dug	-am	hem	rum	pan	hen

No. 15—XV

Jo is my big dog.
Tom is to dig.
Bob had a fig in a bag.
Is my pig fed?
Is not Hal a wag?
Tom had rum in my mug.
He did my sum for me.
Can we go to bed?

We bid him go to bed.
My hog is in mud.
A nag can tug.
A lad had a big jug.
Do not go in to a fen.
A lug of a hog or a pig.
My nag is to be fed.
A mad dog bit a man.

No. 16—XVI. *Words of three Letters. Vowel Short.*

-en	din	-on	hun	gap
ken	fin	con	nun	hap
men	gin	don	pun	lap
pen	kin	-un	run	map
ten	pin	bun	sun	nap
wen	sin	dun	tun	pap
-in	tin	fun	-ap	rap
bin	win	gun	cap	sap

No. 17—XVII. *Words of three Letters. Vowel Short.*

tap	sip	-up	jar	-ur
-ip	tip	cup	mar	cur
dip	-op	pup	par	fur
hip	fop	sup	tar	-as
lip	hop	-ar	war	gas
nip	lop	bar	-or	has
pip	mop	car	for	was
rip	pop	far	nor	-is

No. 18—XVIII. *Words of three Letters. Vowel Short.*

his	mat	get	-it	pit
-us	rat	jet	bit	sit
pus	sat	let	fit	wit
-at	vat	met	hit	-ot
bat	-es	net	kit	cot
cat	yes	pet	lit	dot
fat	-et	set	mit	got
hat	bet	wet	nit	hot

No. 19—XIX. *Words of three Letters. Vowel Short.*

lot	cut	lax	fix	act
not	hut	tax	mix	aft
pot	jut	wax	pix	and
rot	nut	-ex	six	ant
sot	rut	sex	-ox	apt
wot	put (*poot*)	vex	box	ark
-ut	-ax	-ix	fox	arm

No. 20—XX. *Words of three Letters. Vowel Short.*

ask	elm	oft	son (*sun*)
asp	end	urn	ton (*tun*)
elf	imp	her (*hur*)	won (*wun*)
elk	ink	sir (*sur*)	old

Yes: he won my box.
No, sir! it is not so.
He lit a jet of gas.
Mix it all up in a cup.
A rat has bit his leg.
Was it a rat? Oh! no.
Yes: it was a big rat.
A rat has fur on it.

A fir is by his hut.
Put a wad in my gun.
A big fox is in his lot.
Get a gun to hit him.
Oh! my son! do not run so.
It is a hot sun.   Do not go.
A big fox has got my fat hen.
Fix on his cap to fit him.

No. 21—XXI.

A cup is of tin.
It was not my pen.
He set me on a log.
My fan is in a box.
Put on my cap for fun.
Her cap was on his peg.
A fox was in his net.
Run on, for pa is in.
Let him go to get his hat.
Oh! do not hit my cat.

Set his dog on my red fox.
Do not go far; it is wet.
La! he is as fat as a pig.
Put up my map, I beg.
Oh! do not vex me so.
Do not put a cat on a bed.
His lip is cut
Six or ten men sat in a hut.
It is hot : get me a fan.
His hat is on his peg.

No. 22—XXII. Combinations of Syllables in Nos. 1 (I) to 10 (X), to form an easy introduction to words of two Syllables.

READ EVERY SYLLABLE AS IF IT WERE A SEPARATE WORD.
ACCENT ON THE FIRST SYLLABLE.

do'-do	E'-li	ha'-lo	Ca'-to	la'-ic	ti'-ar
fo'-co	Le'-vi	Hu'-go	he'-ro	Ba'-al	bi'-as
lo'-co	ma'-gi	so'-lo	Ne'-ro	di'-al	li'-as
Co'-mo	pe'-ri	Mi'-lo	ty'-ro	vi'-al	Cli'-o
He'-be	Di'-do	Ju'-no	ty'-po	re'-al	ze'-ro
Ca'-di	sa'-go	Ma'-ro	da'-is	li'-ar	ve'-to

No. 23—XXIII. Two Syllables. Accent on the first.

fi'-at	ri'-ot	du'-el	al'-um	ox'-en
di'-et	Bo'-az	fu'-el	at'-om	ax'-is
dy'-er	Bo'-oz	po'-et	po'-em	ev'-er
vi'-ol	Jo'-ab	su'-et	ar'-id	Ar'-ab
li'-on	mo'-ab	ex'-it	Ju'-an	in'-to
Zi'-on	Jo'-el	Ad'-am	ru'-in	un'-to

No. 24—XXIV.

Ma! am I a ty-ro?
O la! it is a ri-ot.
Is Hu-go a li-ar?
Ne-ro is a dy-er.
Is it Ju-no or He-be?
It is my dog Ju-no.
Is Ca-to a he-ro?
A po-em is by a po-et.
An at-om of al-um in a vi-al.
Ad-am! go to my ox-en.

Do not be a li-ar.
A cot is by a ru-in.
Su-et is no di-et.
A man on a li-on.
Ma-ro is a po-et.
A li-ar is a bad man.
Ju-an met a man in a du-el.
He-be is not my dog.
Let us go in-to his hut.
It is an Ar-ab bag.

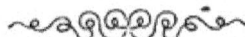

No. 25—XXV   Two Syllables.   Accent on the first.

Y IN THE SECOND SYLLABLE LIKE *E* IN *me*, BUT SHORTER.

CAUTION.—The learner must not say "ba'-*bay*," "To'-*bay*," etc.; but "ba'-*bee*," "To'-*bee*," etc.

ba'-by	ho'-ly	pu'-ny	co-'sy	ha'-zy
To'-by	wi'-ly	ro'-py	po'-sy	la'-zy
ru'-by	du'-ly	Ma'-ry	ro'-sy	ma'-zy
ra'-cy	ug'-ly	va'-ry	mi'-ty	si'-zy
i'-cy	on'-ly	wi'-ry	du'-ty	do'-zy
Lu'-cy	ti'-ny	to'-ry	na'-vy	za'-ny
la'-dy	bo'-ny	fu'-ry	i'-vy	pi'-ny
ti'-dy	po'-ny	ju'-ry	en'-vy	mi'-ry

No. 26—XXVI.   Two Syllables.   Accent on the first.

A IN THE SECOND SYLLABLE LIKE *A* IN *fat*.

CAUTION.—The learner must not say "la'-*ver*," "so'-*der*," etc.; but "la-*vah*," "so-*dah*," etc.

A'-sa	Em'-ma	in'-ca	Ja'-va	Ri'-ga
Ab'-ba	Et'-na	la'-ma	Ju'-ba	Ra'-ca
An'-na	e'-ra	la'-va	Ju'-da	so'-da
Ca'-na	El'-la	Le'-na	Ju'-ra	so'-fa
Cu'-ba	ga'-la	Li'-ma	mi'-ca	to'-ga
El'-ba	Ga'-za	Ly'-ra	pi'-ca	Ve'-ga

No. 27—XXVII.   Accent on the second   Syllable.

a-do' (*doo*)	de-fy'	Ju-ly'	Pe-ru'
a-go'	de-ny'	mam-ma'	to-lu'
al-ly'	du-et'	pa-pa'	up-on'

Lu-cy is a ti-dy la-dy.
It is ug-ly to be in a fu-ry.
Ca-to is in a to-ga.
El-la is to go to Cu-ba.
My po-em is in pi-ca.
It is re-al la-va of Et-na.

Pa-pa is on a ju-ry.
My ti-ny po-ny, if pu-ny, is wi-ry.
Le-na is a ro-sy ba-by.
Is it on-ly To-by?
I do on-ly my du-ty.
It is co-zy to sit on a so-fa.

No. 28—XXVIII.

Words of three Letters, with S added.

web	webs	dog	dogs	cap	caps
rib	ribs	fog	fogs	map	maps
mob	mobs	bug	bugs	lip	lips
rub	rubs	ham	hams	•cup	cups
lad	lads	dim	dims	cat	cats
lid	lids	fan	fans	net	nets
rod	rods	pin	pins	hit	hits
bag	bags	gun	guns	lot	lots
beg	begs	arm	arms	ant	ants
pig	pigs	end	ends	art	arts

It is hot. Ju-ba, run for fans to fan us.

Ma-ry hugs her ba-by in her arms.

My ox-en can tug ten big logs for fu-el.

If a fog dims a Ju-ly sun, it is not so hot.

Tom dips his dog Li-on in a big tub, and wets him.

Lu-cy pins on her hat, and runs to pen up hogs and
pigs.

Oh! do fix my gun, and get me a box of caps.

A sot begs for a mug of rum.

Em-ma hems bags to put rags in.

See Le-na and To-by in a hot sun, and no hats on.

A to-ry ran for his arms, and I got my gun and hit
him.

Sam rubs his po-ny, and sets Tom on him to go and
get a bag of tan.

Ants bit my legs and arms.

1*

SYLLABLES AND WORDS OF THREE AND FOUR LETTERS.

No. 29—XXIX. Syllables. Vowel Long.

bla	ble	bli	blo	blu	bly
cla	cle	cli	clo	clu	cly
fla	fle	fli	flo	flu	fly
gla	gle	gli	glo	glu	gly
pla	ple	pli	plo	plu	ply
sla	sle	shi	slo	slu	sly
bra	bre	bri	bro	bru	bry
cra	cre	cri	cro	cru	cry

No. 30—XXX. Syllables. Vowel Long.

dra	dre	dri	dro	dru	dry
fra	fre	fri	fro	fru	fry
gra	gre	gri	gro	gru	gry
pra	pre	pri	pro	pru	pry
tra	tre	tri	tro	tru	try
wra (*ra*)	wre (*re*)	wri (*ri*)	wro (*ro*)	wru (*ru*)	wry
sha	she	shi	sho	shu	shy
pha (*fa*)	phe (*fe*)	phi (*fi*)	pho (*fo*)	phu (*fu*)	phy

No. 31—XXXI. Syllables. Vowel Long.

ska	ske	ski	sko	sku	sky
sma	sme	smi	smo	smu	smy
sna	sne	sni	sno	snu	sny
spa	spe	spi	spo	spu	spy
sta	ste	sti	sto	stu	sty
swa	swe	swi	swo	swu	swy
dwa	dwe	dwi	dwo	dwu	dwy
qua	que	qui	quo		quy

No. 32—XXXII. *Syllables. Vowel Long.*

scla	scle	scli	sclo	sclu	scly
spla	sple	spli	splo	splu	sply
scra	scre	scri	scro	scru	scry
spra	spre	spri	spro	spru	spry
stra	stre	stri	stro	stru	stry
thra	thre	thri	thro	thru	thry
spha	sphe	sphi	spho	sphu	spby
shra	shre	shri	shro	shru	shry

No. 33—XXXIII.

WORDS—TERMINATIONS Y, EE, OO.

fly	fry	spy	*the*	coo
ply	pry	sty	flee	loo
sly	try	why	glee	too
cry	shy	spry	free	woo
dry	sky	she	*thee*	two (*too*)
			three	who (*hoo*)

A rat was in the tub, and the cat got it.
Oh! see the big fly in my tin cup.
Ten men had guns in the lot.
See the eggs in Tom's hat.
An old elm tree was by the inn.
Try to get the ants off the cups.
Ask who put the pens in the box.
Dry my cap and his hat on the log in the sun.
Her arm was bit by an asp.
Who can get me a tin box for my caps?
Ann has two nuts, and Tom has three.
Try to get the bees on the buds in the lot.
My gun did not go off, for it had no cap.
Three pigs in a sty, and the hog was by.
Why did not Ann fry the ham in the pan?
A sot is not a free man.

Oh ! it is sad for men to be sots.

Let sots fly rum and gin, and be free men.

Bees fly; and so do bats too, but not in the sun.

A sty is for hogs and pigs to be put in.

Ask why Ann sobs so. She has got ink on her map.

See the sly old fox. He robs us of the hens.

An elm is a tree ; and an ash is a tree ; and a fir is
a tree; three trees.

A li-on has cubs; and a hog has pigs; and a dog
has pups.

Lu-cy errs, for she did not do as she was bid.

No. 34—XXXIV

Words of three letters, with the additional syllables

Y, ER, ING.

mad	mad-ly	job	job-ber	sob	sob-bing
sad	sad-ly	rob	rob-ber	wed	wed-ding
mud	mud-dy	rub	rub-ber	dig	dig-ging
dim	dim-ly	gad	gad-der	hem	hem-ming
man	man-ly	bid	bid-der	tan	tan-ning
fen	fen-ny	big	big-ger	win	win-ning
fin	fin-ny	dig	dig-ger	net	net-ting
fun	fun-ny	dim	dim-mer	sit	sit-ting
sun	sun-ny	tan	tan-ner	cut	cut-ting
hap	hap-py	sin	sin-ner	tax	tax-ing
nap	nap-py	win	win-ner	mix	mix-ing
sap	sap-py	gun	gun-ner	fly	fly-ing
pup	pup-py	run	run-ner	cry	cry-ing
jet	jet-ty	dip	dip-per	add	add-ing
fit	fit-ly	up	up-per	ebb	ebb-ing
wit	wit-ly	sup	sup-per	err	err-ing
odd	odd-ly	hat	hat-ter	act	act-ing
apt	apt-ly	cut	cut-ter	end	end-ing

To be wit-ty and fun-ny is not to be hap-py.
En-vy is not man-ly. No sin ev-er is so.
The ba-by was cry-ing for its sup-per.
The net-ting is odd-ly put up. It is too big for the
  bed.
An old man was sit-ting un-der the elm tree, and
  his dog was ly-ing by him.
Tom was dig-ging up the lot to put in hops.
It is too sun-ny for us to be run-ning. Let us sit on
  the log un-der the tree.
A tan-ner has vats or big tubs for tan-ning.
The hat-ter is mat-ting the fur in-to a bat.
See my pup-py and Tom's. Tom's is the big-ger of
  the two.
Lu-cy is add-ing up her sums, and Ka-ty is hem-
  ming.
Al-um is for dy-ers, and so is mad-der. Al-um is
  for fix-ing the dye.
Sam is cut-ting a log for fu-el to get din-ner.

No. 35—XXXV

Words of four and five Letters.   Vowel Short.

blab	dram	snap	quag	class	fall
slab	swam	flat	flax	glass	gall
crab	clan	slat	*chaff*	brass	hall
drab	plan	*chat*	staff	grass	*mall*
stab	bran	*that*	quaff	*char*	pall
clad	scan	flag	*mall*	scar	tall
glad	span	slag	shall	spar	wall
brad	*than*	brag	*bass*	star	small
shad	flap	crag	lass	all	stall
clam	slap	drag	mass	ball	swan
sham	trap	snag	pass	call	what

Words printed in italics have more than one pronunciation. Where
they stand, they are to be pronounced like the words with which they
are classed.

No. 36—XXXVI.

Words of four and five Letters.   *Vowel Short.*

bled	*th*em	dell	dwell	tress	brim
fled	glen	fell	swell	glib	grim
sled	*th*en	sell	less	crib	prim
sped	when	tell	mess	drib	trim
shed	step	well	bless	slid	swim
bred	fret	smell	cress	brig	whim
dreg	bell	spell	dress	whig	grin
stem	*c*ell	quell	press	slim	spin

No. 37—XXXVII.

Words of four and five Letters.   *Vowel Short.*

thin	quip	cliff	pill	skill	bliss
clip	whip	whiff	rill	still	swiss
slip	*th*is	bill	sill	swill	clod
trip	flit	fill	till	quill	plod
drip	slit	*gill*	will	shrill	trod
grip	grit	hill	*ch*ill	hiss	clog
*ch*ip	quit	kill	drill	kiss	flog
ship	whit	mill	frill	miss	frog

No. 38—XXXVIII.

Words of four and five Letters.   *Vowel Short.*

from	shot	cross	shrug	spur	bluff	mull
crop	trot	dross	drum	shut	gruff	null
drop	spot	floss	plum	*th*us	*ch*uff	skull
shop	doff	gloss	scum	buff	snuff	bunn
slop	scoff	club	*ch*um	cuff	stuff	burr
prop	doll	drub	swum	huff	cull	purr
stop	loll	grub	spun	luff	dull	buss
blot	loss	shrub	stun	muff	gull	fuss
plot	moss	snug	shun	puff	hull	buzz
grot	toss	drug	blur	ruff	lull	fuzz

EXCEPTIONS.

O long.			*U=OO*	
boll	roll	scroll	bull	pull
poll	toll	gross	full	puss

I see two or three tall lads in the hall.
Let us go and cull the buds on the hill ; we will get
  hats full and laps full of them.
The bell tolls, and we will go.
Get me my muff, and I will go too.
Let us pass by the well, and fill the cups.
The big dogs will kill all the rats.
Do not put ink on my doll's cuffs.
I will kiss my doll, and put her to bed.
The man gets toll at the mill.
Let puss sit by us, and she will purr.
Oh! let us run, and roll the balls on the hill.
Tell me who has the bunns for us.
Shall we go to see the ship and the two brigs?
Yes: we will go in that skiff, and put up a flag.
Ann shall dress: she will be glad to go too.
A swan was shot by a lad at that cliff.
It is a bad plan to sit on the wet grass.
My doll is snug in her crib: do not stir, doll.
This doll frets: shall I whip her if she is not still?
Put that ox in this stall: I will get him bran and
  slops.
Old Tom has a small shop in that shed.
Drag the sled up to the steps till we get on it.
She shall spell in his class, and then she shall get a
  plum.
I had a glass pen: it had no slit in it. I will get a
  quill pen: that is not so stiff.
A hog can not swim well; but a dog can.

No. 39--XXXIX.

Words of four and five Letters, with the additional syllables, ER *and* ING. *To be spelled and read across.*

blab	blab-ber	blab-bing	brim	brim-mer	brim-ming
plan	plan-ner	plan-ning	swim	swim-mer	swim-ming
scan	scan-ner	scan-ning	spin	spin-ner	spin-ning
span	span-ner	span-ning	clip	clip per	clip-ping
flap	flap-per	flap-ping	slip	slip-per	slip-ping
slap	slap-per	slap-ping	trip	trip-per	trip-ping
snap	snap-per	snap-ping	ship	ship-per	ship-ping
chat	*chat-ter*	*chat-ting*	stop	stop-per	stop-ping
brag	brag-ger	brag-ging	blot	blot-ter	blot-ting
drag	drag-ger	drag-ging	plot	plot-ter	plot-ting
spell	spell-er	spell-ing	trot	trot-ter	trot-ting
dwell	dwell-er	dwell-ing	drum	drum-mer	drum-ming
dress	dress-er	dress-ing	shut	shut-ter	shut-ting

Em-ma can spell in my class. She is spell-ing and add-ing.

Le-na was in to see us. She is get-ting to be a tall la-dy.

See the flag flap-ping on the top of that tall crag.

Lu-cy was dress-ing her doll, when I was trim-ming my dress.

My po-ny is pull-ing the sled. Do not whip him.

As I was pass-ing the mill, I fell in the mud.

See what a big bug I trod on. Tom is kill-ing it.

That old man has snuff in a box. See; he is snuff-ing.

It is ug-ly to be loll-ing. Do not be so la-zy.

The bell is toll-ing. Let us get sup-per and go to bed.

El-la was toss-ing her ball, when she fell in the wet grass.

Sam is call-ing us to din-ner. Let us all dress and go.

Get logs to prop that wall. It is fall-ing.

I was fill-ing my tin cup from the dip-per at the well.

Fan-ny is hem-ming her frill bad-ly. She is in a hur-ry.

The mil-ler was sell-ing grits and bran at the mill.

No. 40.—XL.

Words of two Syllables, accented on the first. Two Consonants between the Syllables. The Vowel in the accented Syllable short.

ad der	far *ther*	mut ter	stam mer	whis per
af ter	fes ter	num ber	suf fer	wil der
al der	fet ter	of fer	sum mer	win ner
am ber	fil ter	or der	sun der	win ter
ant ler	flat ter	pat ter	sup per	won der
arc*h* er	flut ter	pep per	sut ler	(*wun der*)
ban ner	fod der	pes ter	tat ter	beg gar
ban ter	for mer	plun der	tat tler	col lar
bar ter	frit ter	pon der	tem per	dol lar
bat ter	gar ter	pot ter	ten der	gram mar
bet ter	gen der	prof fer	tet ter	med lar
bit ter	gin *ger*	pros per	thun der	mor tar
blad der	glit ter	quar ter	tim ber	nec tar
blis ter	ham mer	raf ter	tin der	pil lar
blub ber	ham per	ram bler	tot ter	stel lar
blun der	hin der	ren der	trig ger	vul gar
bor der	lad der	rud der	tum bler	doc tor
but ter	let ter	scam per	ul cer	er ror
*ch*ar ter	lim ner	scat ter	um ber	fac tor
*ch*at ter	lit ter	shel ter	un der	mir ror
cob bler	lub ber	shud der	up per	par lor
cop per	lum ber	shut ter	ush er	pas tor
cor ner	mas ter	sil ver	ut ter	rec tor
cum ber	mat ter	sim per	ver ger	spon sor
dag ger	mem ber	slan der	ves per	sculp tor
dap per	mer cer	slen der	vint ner	suc cor
dif fer	mil ler	slip per	wan der	vic tor
el der	min ster	slum ber	war bler	li quor
en ter	mon ster	smat ter	war der	(*lick er*)
fal ter	mur der	squan der	wel ter	mur mur

No. 41.—XLI.

The cob-bler sits in his stall, and ham-mers on and on.

He stops but to get his din-ner or supper.

I will try not to blun-der when I spell.

Go and get fod der for the ox-en. If an ox is not well fed, the far mer's crops will suf fer.

The men will mus-ter in the big lot at the cor-ner, in or der to en-ter the ar-my.

The man who squan-ders will be a beg gar.

A stag has an-tlers, but an ox has not.

Do not pull the trig-ger of that gun. It will go off.

A gram-mar can not be got for a quar ter of a dol-lar.

See the tall mir-ror on the wall in the par-lor.

Get the ham-pers from the shed, and put the win-ter fod-der in them.

Let us go and cut tim-ber for raf-ters, and get mor-tar to plaster the shed.

Do not stam-mer and fal-ter so in spell-ing.

Lu-cy had a blis-ter on her arm. The doc-tor put it on, and she suf-fers from it.

Do not hinder him. He will blun-der in spell-ing his let-ter, and blot it.

What a small slip-per Em-ma has! It is too small for her.

See the big fly in that sil-ver cup. How he is buzz-ing!

What num-ber of tum-blers has Tom-my got in that big ham-per?

ban ner	ban ners	scat ter	scat ters
cor ner	cor ners	shel ter	shel ters
fet ter	fet ters	ut ter	ut 'ters
ham mer	ham mers	won der	won ders
let ter	let ters	beg gar	beg gars
mem ber	mem bers	pil lar	pil lars
mer cer	mer cers	rec tor	rec tors
num ber	num bers	spon sor	spon-sors
of fer	of fers	sculp tor	sculp tors
quar ter	quarters	mur mur	mur murs

No. 42.—XLII.

Words of two Syllables accented on the first. Two consonants between the Syllables. The Vowel in the accented Syllable short.

at'-tic	lob'-by	wher'-ry	er' rant	min'-strel
bal'-lot	mer'-cy	fren'-zy	ex'-tant	mor'-sel
bar'-ren	moss'-y	gris'-ly	flip'-pant	par'-cel
bas'-ket	pal'-sy	griz'-zly	gal'-lant-	quar'-rel
bil'-let	pan'-try	hur'-ry	in'-stant	satch'-el
bod'-kin	par'-ty	ac'-cent	mor' dant	sor'-rel
bon'-net	pet'-ty	ad'-vent	pen'-nant	squir'-rel
buf'-fet	pret'-ty	ar'-dent	quad'-rant	tram'-mel
cam'-let	(prit-ty)	com'-ment	ram'-pant	tun'-nel
cob'-web	prox'-y	con'-vent	reg'-nant	tim'-brel
crim'-son	put'-ty	cres'-cent	rem'-nant	ves'-sel
cul'-prit	quar'-ry	cur'-rent	scr'-vant	her'-bal
des'-pot	quin'-sy	fer'-ment	sex'-tant	mar'-shal
ar'-my	scan'-ty	gar'-ment	stag'-nant	men'-tal
ban'-dy	scur'-vy	lam'-bent	ver'-dant	mor'-tal
bel'-fry	sen'-try	pun'-gent	war'-rant	ras'-cal
ber'-ry	six'-ty	seg'-ment	hus'-band	rent'-al
can'-dy	sor'-ry	scr'-pent	bar'-rel	sig'-nal
cler'-gy	sul'-ly	sol'-vent	can'-cel	ver'-bal
clum'-sy	sul'-try	strin'-gent	chan'-cel	ver'-nal
dit'-ty	sun'-dry	tan'-gent	chan'-nel	ves'-tal
ed'-dy	swarth'-y	tor'-ment	dam'-sel	an'-vil
en'-vy	tal'-ly	tor'-rent	fen'-nel	fos'-sil
fer'-ry	tar'-dy	vest'-ment	flan'-nel	nos'-tril
fif'-ty	tar'-ry	ar'-rant	fun'-nel	pen'-cil
flim'-sy	thir'-ty	con'-stant	gos'-pel	ton'-sil
gip'-sy	tip'-sy	des'-cant	ken'-nel	gam'-bol
jel'-ly	twen'-ty	dis'-tant	ker'-nel	pis'-tol
jol'-ly	ves'-try	dor'-mant	mar'-vel	sym'-bol

Get a bil-let from the bas-ket, and put it on.
What a pret-ty bon-net Ma-ry has got!
Fan-ny has a cam-let dress.
Flan-nel is for win-ter gar-ments.
A cob-web is wo-ven by a spi-der.

No. 43—XLIII.

*A single consonant between the Vowels in the two
Syllables. The Vowel in the accented Syllable
short.*

CAUTION.—Do not spell *cop-py* for *cop-y*, *bod-dy*
for *bod-y*, etc.

ev'-er	plov'-er	rig'-or	ten-'ant	cav'-il
nev'-er	fath'-er	val'-or	preb'-end	civ'-il
sev'-er	rath'-er	vig'-or	ger'-und	per'-il
clev'-er	neth'-er	vis'-or	cam'-el	vig'-il
leg'-er	teth'-er	lev'-y	chis'-el	cor'-al
giv'-er	weth'-er	ver'-y	chap'-el	med'-al
liv'-er	wheth'-er	lil'-y	grav'-el	met'-al
quiv'-er	hith'-er	pit'-y	bev'-el	mor'-al
riv'-er	whith'-er	bod'-y	lev'-el	ped'-al
shiv'-er	oth'-er	cop'-y	mod'-el	car'-ol
prim'-er	moth'-er	cem'-ent	nov'-el	cred'-it
prop'-er	broth'-er	pat'-ent	pan'-el	hab'-it
cov'-er	zeph'-yr	pres'-ent	rav'-el	lim'-it
hov'-er	schol'-ar	tal'-ent	rev'-el	spir'-it
lov'-er	vic'-ar	ped'-ant	trav'-el	crit'-ic

Tell the ser-vant to kill the big tur-key for din-ner.
Do not tar-ry in go-ing on an er-rand.
We will cross the fer-ry, and we can car-ry a bar-
rel to get grav-el for the gar-den.
Af-ter a rev-el is a quar-rel, when the par-ty get
tip-sy on whis-key.
A man from fif-ty to six-ty is get-ting old.
Twen-ty is two tens; thir-ty is three tens; six-ty is
six tens.
Cov-er the prim-er, or it will get too dir ty.
Tom-my will kill a squir-rel, and we will get it for
din-ner.
I had rath-er be a gip-sy, and wan-der free if but a
beg-gar, than be the ser-vant of a ty-rant, and be
in con-stant per-il from his tem-per.
It is a pit-y to see a schol-ar and a man of tal-ent go
to ru-in by li-quor.

Set me a cop-y, and let me get a pen-cil or ink and a
pen, and try what I can do.

Do not swim in the chan-nel of the riv-er. See how
the cur-rent runs. It can car-ry off the skiff, if
we let it go.

The gal-lant flag is fly-ing on the flag-staff in the
zeph-yr.

Mor-tar is the cem-ent for walls; but it will not do
for glass.

In "cem-ent," if we put the ac-cent on cem, what is
it? Cem'-ent. But if we put the ac-cent on ment,
what is it? Ce-ment'

No. 44—XLIV.

Silent E lengthens the preceding Vowel.

lad	lade	car	care	hid	hide	con	cone
mad	made	far	fare	rid	ride	hop	hope
sam	same	mar	mare	dim	dime	mop	mope
can	cane	par	pare	din	dine	for	fore
fan	fane	tar	tare	fin	fine	dot	dote
man	mane	bat	bate	kin	kine	not	note
pan	pane	fat	fate	pin	pine	rot	rote
van	vane	hat	hate	win	wine	cub	cube
cap	cape	mat	mate	rob	robe	tub	tube
nap	nape	pat	pate	nod	node	tun	tune
tap	tape	rat	rate	rod	rode	cur	cure
bar	bare	bid	bide	top	tope	cut	cute

Tell the *lad* to *lade* the nag.
The hot sum-mer *made* the dog *mad.*
Sam is not the *same* lad that he was.
Can I not get a *cane* to whip the po-ny?
The *man* was cut-ting the po-ny's *mane.*
That *pan* is made of tin. A *pane* is made of glass.
Tom had a fur *cap,* and a *cape.*
I *hid* my box of eggs. Ann can *hide* hers.
I *hate* to put on an old *hat.*
Lu-cy *rode* the nag, and she had no *rod.*
I had *not* got Ann's *note* till it was too late.

No. 45—XLV

Silent E lengthens the preceding Vowel and softens C and G.

babe	space	trade	bake	flake	pale
ace	trace	safe	cake	shake	sale
face	fade	chafe	lake	snake	tale
lace	jade	age	make	stake	vale
mace	wade	cage	rake	ale	scale
pace	blade	page	take	bale	stale
race	glade	rage	sake	dale	whale
brace	grade	sage	wake	gale	came
grace	shade	wage	brake	hale	dame
place	spade	stage	drake	male	fame

No. 46—XLVI.

game	dane	scrape	case	grate	save
lame	lane	dare	chase	prate	wave
name	sane	hare	vase	skate	brave
same	wane	glare	phrase	slate	crave
tame	crane	scare	ate	cave	grave
blame	ape	share	date	gave	shave
flame	crape	snare	gate	lave	slave
frame	scape	spare	late	nave	stave
shame	grape	square	crate	pave	gaze
bane	shape	base	plate	rave	haze

No. 47—XLVII.

maze	these	nice	side	life	pile
graze	mete	rice	tide	wife	tile
glebe	eve	vice	wide	strife	vile
eke	gibe	price	bride	like	wile
theme	bribe	slice	chide	pike	smile
scheme	tribe	spice	glide	spike	while
scene	scribe	splice	pride	strike	style
here	ice	trice	slide	bile	lime
mere	dice	twice	stride	file	time
sphere	mice	thrice	fife	mile	chime

No. 48—XLVIII.

clime	brine	ripe	sire	cite	dive
prime	chine	type	tire	mite	five
slime	shine	wipe	wire	rite	rive
crime	spine	gripe	quire	site	drive
dime	thine	stripe	spire	smite	strive
lime	whine	snipe	squire	spite	thrive
mine	swine	dire	lyre	trite	size
nine	twine	fire	rise	quite	prize
pine	shrine	hire	wise	white	lobe
vine	pipe	mire	bite	sprite	globe

No. 49—XLIX.

probe	woke	sole	prone	bore	score
ode	yoke	dome	stone	core	shore
bode	broke	home	throne	gore	store
code	choke	tome	cope	lore	swore
mode	smoke	bone	pope	more	dose
strode	spoke	hone	rope	pore	close
doge	stroke	lone	grope	sore	hose
coke	hole	tone	scope	tore	nose
joke	mole	zone	trope	wore	pose
poke	pole	drone	ore	yore	rose

No. 50—L.

chose	cove	strove	huge	spume	sure
prose	rove	throve	duke	june	(shoor)
those	wove	doze	luke	lune	use
mote	clove	froze	mule	prune	muse
vote	drove	truce	rule	dupe	lute
smote	grove	spruce	fume	lure	mute
quote	stove	rude	plume	pure	flute

Exceptions pronounced nearly as they would be without the silent E.		O like U in Us.		O like U in Full.	
are	give	come	none	lose	move
bade	live	some	dove	whose	prove
gape	gone	one	glove	E like A in Fate.	
have	shone	(wun)	love	ere	where
		done	shove	there	

Words Unclassified.

buy (by)	you (u)	ewe (u)
been (bin)	your (ure)	eye (i)

No. 51—LI.

Will you sit here, while we go to the well there?
Shall we not get some fire for the stove?
Oh! it will be nice to have a slide on the ice.
If you have your skates, let us skate there like
   those men.
No : do not be so brave; for you will fall in a trice.
Will you strive to shake off some of those ripe
   grapes?
O yes! come and I will give you one or two of them.
Where are your gloves? Your ma bade you put
   them on.
See the stars and bars on that flag.
A score is two times ten, or twice ten.
White makes a nice dress in the hot sum-mer.
Five times six and three times ten are the same.
The smoke is bad for one's eyes.
Will you buy me some twine to fly my kite?
Vice can make a man like a brute.
Cloves and mace are spice.
Why did you strike the mule on the nose?
The ram is the male of the ewe.
Whose store shall we go to, to buy a grate?
Come and see the li-on. You have not been there.
Prove your love by acts.

No. 52—LII.

—ED and —ING ; to be read and spelled across.

CAUTION.—Make the final *d* very distinct.

wage	waged	wa'-ging	dare	dared	da'-ring
scale	scaled	sca'-ling	scare	scared	sca'-ring
name	named	na'-ming	shave	shaved	sha'-ving
tame	tamed	ta'-ming	spare	spared	spa'-ring
blame	blamed	bla'-ming	pave	paved	pa'ving
frame	framed	fra'-ming	save	saved	sa'-ving
shame	shamed	sha'-ming	crave	craved	cra'-ving
wane	waned	wa'-ning	gaze	gazed	ga'-zing

No. 53—LIII.

bribe	bribed	bri-bing	bore	bored	bo ring
file	filed	fi-ling	pore	pored	po-ring
pile	piled	pi-ling	close	closed	clo sing
smile	smiled	smi-ling	rove	roved	ro ving
chime	chimed	chi ming	doze	dozed	do zing
line	lined	li ning	rule	ruled	ru ling
twine	twined	twi ning	prune	pruned	pru ning
hire	hired	hi-ring	lure	lured	lu ring
tire	tired	ti ring	use	used	u sing

No. 54—LIV

D=T.

face	faced	fa cing	wake	waked	wa king
lace	laced	la cing	shape	shaped	sha ping
pace	paced	pa cing	scrape	scraped	scra ping
race	raced	ra cing	chase	chased	cha sing
brace	braced	bra cing	slice	sliced	sli cing
grace	graced	gra cing	spice	spiced	spi-cing
place	placed	pla cing—	stripe	striped	stri ping
trace	traced	tra cing	joke	joked	jo king
bake	baked	ba king	smoke	smoked	smo king
rake	raked	ra king	grope	groped	gro ping

No. 55—LV

fade	fa-ded	fa-ding	plate	pla ted	pla ting
jade	ja ded	ja ding	prate	pra ted	pra ting
wade	wa ded	wa ding	skate	ska ted	ska ting
shade	sha ded	sha ding	mete	me ted	me ting
trade	tra ded	tra ding	glide	gli ded	gli ding
date	da ted	da ting	quote	quo ted	quo ting

S making an additional Syllable.

face	fa ces	trace	tra ces	vice	vi ces
lace	la ces	age	a ges	price	pri ces
pace	pa-ces	cage	ca ges	slice	sli ces
race	ru ces	page	pa ges	spice	spi-ces
brace	bra ces	stage	sta ges	dose	do ses
grace	gra ces.	case	ca ses	nose	no-ses
place	pla ces	vase	va ses	truce	tru ces
space	spa ces	phrase	phra ses	use	u ses

No. 56—LVI.

ER, EST, LY.

safe	sa-fer	sa-fest	safe-ly
sage	sa-ger	sa-gest	sage-ly
lame	la-mer	la-mest	lame-ly
base	ba-ser	ba-sest	base-ly
late	la-ter	la test	late-ly
brave	bra-ver	bra-vest	brave-ly
grave	gra-ver	gra-vest	grave-ly
nice	ni-cer	ni-cest	nice-ly
wide	wider	wi-dest	wide-ly
ripe	ri-per	ri-pest	ripe-ly
wise	wi-ser	wi-sest	wise-ly
sore	so-rer	so-rest	sore-ly
close	clo-ser	clo-sest	close-ly
rude	ru-der	ru-dest	rude-ly
huge	hu-ger	hu-gest	huge-ly
pure	pu-rer	pu-rest	pure ly
sure	su-rer	su-rest	surely
fine	fi-ner	fi-nest	fine-ly

No. 57—LVII.

The ba-by wakes: see, it is smi ling.

The ox-en are gra-zing in the lot. Let us drive them home.

These cakes are nice-ly baked. Will you have some?

Tell Lu cy to cut some sli ces of ham for sup per.

Tom ska-ted o ver the lake on the ice.

We have spell ed ten pa ges in no long time.

In old times there were nine Mu-ses, and three Gra ces, and three Fates.

Sure-ly it is wi sest to be sa ving in time, so as to have some thing if we are spared to be old.

The man that pa hired has been pru-ning the grape vines, and we shall have more grapes.

Do not sit so close by the fire; your dress is smo-
king.
If you can spell *tame*, you can sure-ly spell *tamed*,
and *ta-mer*, and *ta-ming*, and *tame ly*.
See the white swan gli-ding to the shore of the
lake: note its grace as it moves.
I will ask ma to buy me that ti ny doll that moves
its eyes so: and then I will dress it, oh! so
nice ly.
Do not pull the grapes. Let them get ri-per.
You must not blame oth ers for your er-rors.

No. 58—LVIII.

Two Syllables. Accent on first.

CAUTION.—The last syllable must be distinctly
uttered. Do not say fa-*tl* for fa-*tal*, or pu-*pl* for pu-
pil, or fe'-*vah* for fe'-*ver*. Distinguish the words in *ey*
from those in *y*.

sha'-dy	bar'-ley	mon'-ey	cri'-er	ve'-nal
gra'-vy	chim'-ney	(*mun*)	pli'-er	fi'-nal
cra'-zy	cov'-ey	mon'-key	go'-er	spi'-nal
que'-ry	(*kuv*)	(*mung*)	pri'-or	pa'-pal
bri'-ny	gal'-ley	pars'-ley	cru'-et	spi'-ral
spi'-cy	hack'-ney	pul'-ley	qui'-et	mu'-ral
sli'-ly	hon-ey	tur'-key	ne'-gro	ru'-ral
sli'-my	(*hun*)	val'-ley	fo'-cal	su'-ral
cro'-ny	jer'-sey	vol'-ley	lo'-cal	cru'-ral
sto'-ny	jock'-ey	whis'-key	vo'-cal	plu'-ral
glo'-ry	kid'-ney	flu'-id	du'-cal	na'-sal
sto'-ry	lack'-ey	cru'-el	ti'-dal	fa'-tal
tru'-ly	lam'-prey	gru'-el	bri'-dal	an'-y
ab'-bey	med'-ley	bru'-in	le'-gal	(*en*)
al'-ley	mot'-ley	fri'-ar	re'-gal	man'-y
par'-ley	pal'-frey	bri'-er	pe'-nal	(*men*)

No. 59—LIX. ER=UR.

na'-tal	hu'-man	tu'-ber	wa'-ger	dra'-per
pe'-tal	pa'-gan	di'-cer	ba'-ker	scra'-per
vi'-tal	sa'-tan	pa'-cer	ma'-ker	ti'-ler
to'-tal	ce'-dar.	ra'-cer	ra'-ker	mi'-ner
o'-val	su'-gar	gro'-cer	qua'-ker	pi'-per
na'-val	(shŏo)	ci'-der	po'-ker	vi'-per
ri'-val.	mo'-lar	ri'-der	jo'-ker	to'-per
ba'-bel	po'-lar	spi'-der	bro'-ker	tu'-ner
la'-bel	so'-lar	fi'-fer	fra'-mer	ru'-ler
li'-bel	lu'-nar	wa'-fer	ca'-per	sche'-mer
pu'-pil	la'-zar	tra'-der	pa' per	lov'-er
e'-vil	so'-ber	ti'-ger	ta'-per	(luv)

No. 60—LX.

mi-ser	me-ter	dro-ver	pi-lot	man-ger
ri-ser	fe-ver	do-nor	cu-bic	ran-ger
ca-ter	le-ver	ma-jor	cu-bit	stran-ger
gra-ter	e-ther	stu-por.	tu-lip	tip-pler
sla-ter	di-ver	ju-ror	lù-cid	fid-dler
gra-ver	dri-ver	tu-tor	mu-sic	sad-dler
sla-ver	ci-pher	ra-zor	stu-pid	sol-dier
sha-ver	o-ver	i-tem	hu-mid	(sole-jér)
wa-ver	ro-ver	o-men	cham-ber	los'-er
qua-ver	clo-ver	re-bus	dan-ger	(looz'-er)

Oh! what a fine fat ba-by! Let me kiss it.

Set it on the po-ny to take a ride.

Drive to the sha-dy lane, and we will sit on the grass.

Do not take the la-bel off that vi-al.

Make the ne-gro kill that spi-der.

Get me a ru-ler to rule that pa-per.

Wa-fers are for clo-sing let-ters.

It is fa-tal to a tra-der to be a li-ar.
It is sa-fer nev-er to tell a sto-ry.
A li-òn is bra-ver than a ti-ger.
Do not be so la-zy: it is a fa-tal vice.
A gro-cer sells su-gar, and a ba-ker makes cakes.
A di-al tells the time by the sun.
Take the po-ker and rake that fire.
An o-val is of the shape of an egg.
Add *ly* to *qui-et*, and you make *qui-et-ly*.
We will see if you can spell some more like it.

No. 61—LX1.

Easy Words of three Syllables. Accented on the first.

CAUTION.—Say lo-*cal*, not lo-*kl*; o-*ral*, not o-*rl*;
fa-*tal*, not fa-*tl*, etc.

cru-el	cru-el-ly	o-ral	o-ral-ly
cru-el	cru-el-ty	spi-ral	spi-ral-ly
qui-et	qui-et-ly	ru-ral	ru-ral-ly
lo cal	lo-cal-ly	fa-tal	fa-tal-ly
vo-cal	vo-cal-ly	vi-tal	vi-tal-ly
le-gal	le-gal-ly	to-tal	to-tal-ly
re-gal	re-gal-ly	ri-val	ri-val-ry
pe-nal	pe-nal-ly	mi-ser	mi-serly
ve-nal	ve-nal-ly	stu-pid	stu-pid-ly
fi-nal	fi-nal-ly	hu-mid	hu-mid-ly
am-ity	hom-ily	am-u-let	bar-o-net
bar-on-y	nov-el-ty	a-pri-cot	ban-ner-et
com-i-ty	par-i-ty	ben-e-fit	cas-ta-net
dim-i-ty	pu-ri-ty	cab-i-net	char-i-ot
eb-o-ny	qual-i-ty	lev-er-et	cov-er-let
ev-er-y	ra-ri-ty	min-a-ret	(*kuv*)
fi ner-y	san-i-ty	par-a-pet	cor-o-net
gun-ner-y	u-ni-ty	pa-tri-ot	el-e-ment

No. 62—LXII.

LCH=LSH; NCH=NSH; TCH=TSH.

CAUTION.—Be careful to sound the final d. Do not say *ban* for *band*, etc.

band	wind	wing	sung	clench	scorch
hand	bond	bring	clung	drench	lurch
land	fond	cling	flung	quench	church
sand	blond	fling	slung	trench	batch
bland	fund	sling	stung	finch	catch
brand	held	sting	sprung	linch	hatch
stand	gild	thing	strung	pinch	latch
strand	herd	swing	swung	winch.	match
gland	curd	spring	rich	clinch	patch
grand	surd	string	which	flinch	thatch
bend	bulb	long	much	bunch	snatch
lend	curb	song	such	lunch	scratch
mend	pelf	prong	belch	munch	fetch
rend	self	thong	filch	punch	sketch
send	shelf	throng	milch	larch	stretch
tend	turf	strong	branch	march	ditch
vend	scurf	bung	cranch	parch	fetch
wend	king	hung	stanch	starch	hitch
blend	ring	lung	bench	perch	pitch
spend	sing	rung	blench	torch	witch

There is a bunch of nice grapes on that shelf.
The finch sings his song on the perch of his cage.
The sol-dier's life, in the time of war, is a life of dan-ger.
You can save mon-ey, and not be mi-ser-ly.
A ci-pher af-ter a num-ber makes it ten times more.
A fine schol-ar is rare-ly a ped-ant.
Ev-er-y hu-man be ing is mor-tal.
Mon ey is, in man-y ca ses, more than a ri-val of God.

No. 63—LXIII.

flitch	flash	path	check	block	silk
stitch	trash	depth	speck	clock	bulk
switch	smash	pith	lick	crock	hulk
twitch	splash	with	nick	flock	link
sylph	mesh	frith	pick	frock	pink
nymph	flesh	myth	rick	shock	sink
botch	fresh	smith	sick	stock	wink
notch	dish	filth	tick	buck	blink
blotch	fish	plinth	wick	duck	brink
clutch	wish	tenth	brick	luck	ink
crutch	gush	length	click	suck	link
cash	hush	strength	quick	tuck	pink
dash	mush	troth	stick	cluck	drink
gash	rush	moth	trick	pluck	slink
hash	blush	broth	chick	stuck	think
lash	brush	froth	thick	struck	shrink
mash	crush	cloth	dock	chuck	drunk
rash	flush	beck	lock	elk	slunk
sash	bath	deck	mock	welk	trunk
clash	hath	neck	rock	whelk	shrunk
crash	lath	peck	sock	milk	jerk

No. 64—LXIV

sept	wert	rest	crest	tost	rust
wept	sort	test	drest	frost	crust
crept	short	vest	fist	dust	trust
slept	hurt	west	list	bust	burst
swept	best	zest	mist	gust	durst
tempt	lest	quest	midst	just	minx
crypt	nest	blest	cost	lust	(m'ngks)
pert	pest	chest	lost	must	lynx
					(l'ngks)

No. 65—LXV.

A in *ask, spasm, pant*, and similar words, is between
a in *far* and *a* in *fat*.

*clerk	curl	help	thump	belt	pent
cork	furl	scalp	stump	felt	rent
fork	hurl	gulp	spasm	melt	sent
stork	purl	pulp	chasm	pelt	tent
lurk	churl	camp	lisp	dwelt	vent
turk	elm	damp	crisp	smelt	went
ask	helm	lamp	cusp	gilt	spent
bask	film	clamp	fact	hilt	dint
cask	term	cramp	tact	quilt	hint
mask	sperm	tramp	tract	tilt	lint
task	fern	hemp	sect	wilt	mint
desk	stern	imp	strict	cant	tint
disk	born	limp	duct	pant	flint
risk	corn	crimp	heft	rant	print
brisk	horn	pomp	left	chant	squint
frisk	morn	romp	lift	grant	stint
whisk	scorn	bump	sift	plant	font
dusk	urn	dump	drift	scant	hunt
husk	burn	lump	loft	slant	blunt
musk	turn	pump	soft	bent	brunt
rusk	churn	clump	croft	cent	kept
tusk	spurn	plump	tuft	lent	celt

A vi-per is a small snake. The sting of a bee is not
so bad as the bite of a vi-per.
A moth will cut holes in cloth, and ru-in it.
An ox is fond of clo-ver; but a li-on or a ti-ger is
fond of flesh.

[* " *Clerk* and *Sergeant* are uniformly pronounced *Clark* and *Sar-
geant* by the English orthœpists; but in this country it is very com-
mon to pronounce them, in accordance with their orthography, with
the sound of the *e* as in *jerk*."—WORCESTER.]

The land which we till is rich: it brings corn for us,
and for the ne-groes, and for a herd of mules.
I think a tu-lip has much fi-ner tints than a rose;
but then it has no smell like the rose.
Get me a long rod with a long string at the end of
it, and let me catch fish,—rock and perch. I like
them so much, and it will be such fun.
A bunch of grapes hung o-ver me, and I sprung up
to catch it,—but I on-ly tore my dress.
I wish I were not so late a ri-ser: it makes me so
stu-pid.

No. 66—LXVI.

Haft, gasp, past, and similar words, have the *a* be-
tween *a* in *far* and *a* in *fat.* In *fir* and the words
following, *i=e* in *men.*

bang	frank	track	past	carp	hark
fang	plank	haft	vast	harp	lark
gang	prank	raft	blast	sharp	mark
hang	shrank	waft	barb	cart	park
pang	thank	craft	garb	dart	shark
rang	back	draft	bard	hart	spark
sang	hack	graft	card	mart	stark
clang	lack	shaft	guard	part	fir
slang	nack	gasp	hard	tart	(fer)
twang	pack	grasp	lard	chart	dirk
bank	rack	clasp	yard	smart	kirk
dank	sack	bask	scarf	start	smirk
hank	tack	cask	marl	larch	quirk
lank	black	mask	snarl	march	gird
rank	crack	task	farm	parch	girl
sank	quack	cast	harm	starch	whirl
tank	slack	fast	charm	harsh	twirl
blank	snack	hast	barn	marsh	firm
crank	stack	last	darn	lark	chirp
drank	smack	mast	tarn	dark	skirt

No. 67—LXVII. '

In •the first five words, *i*==*e* in *men.* In the nine following words, *i*==*u* in *us.*

squirt	doth	dwarf	bold	port
birth	dost	swarm	cold	sport
firth	does	hash	fold	host
girth	(*duz*)	asp	hold	post
mirth	worth	hasp	sold	most
sir (*sur*)	thrall	grasp	told	g(h)ost
stir	squall	wasp	wold	pork
bird	bald	clasp	scold	both
third	scald	wast	poll	loth
shirt	halt	watch	toll	sloth
spirt	malt	quash	(k)noll	forth
bir*ch*	salt	mild	droll	por*ch*
first	want	wild	stroll	quoth
thi*r*st	swan	*ch*ild	scroll	
word	ward	bind	bolt	
world	sward	find	colt	
work	wart	hind	dolt	U *as in* FULL
wort	quart	kind	jolt	put
wont	thwart	mind	ford	puss
front	warm	rind	fort	bush
worm	warń	wind	torn	push
monk	warp	blind	worn	ruth
month	wharf	grind	sworn	truth

My old hat is bad-ly worn, but I am loth to part
with it.
See the i-vy: it runs all o-ver the porch.
We want some ri-per grapes than these. Let us
stroll qui-et-ly back, and pluck them off the vines.
Oh ! what a fine pa-cer that colt will be !
That stu-pid ne-gro girl fell in the dirt with the child.

A hog ran past, and gave her a push when she was
  off her guard.
Put a scarf on my neck, and I will be a po-ny, and
  trot in the yard.
Put on a white shirt and a mask, and you can be
  a ghost when it is dark.
I will not do such a thing; for that is cru-el sport.
It will be bet-ter fun to march to mu-sic, and we can
  halt and form a line on the sward in front of the
  gate.

No. 68—LXVIII.

E softens the preceding C or G. In *dance, basque,*
and similar words, *a* is between *a* in *far* and *a* in
fat.

dance	sense	wedge ·	hinge	mosqué
lance	tense	dredge	plunge	(*mosk*)
glance	lapse	midge	barge	valve
chance	glimpse	ridge	large	delve
pounce	parse	bridge	charge	twelve
trance	sparse	dodge	merge	solve
fence	terse	lodge	serge	carve
hence	verse	budge	verge	starve
pence	corse	fudge	dirge	nerve
thence	horse	judge	(*durge*)	serve
whence	curse	drudge	basque	sponge
mince	nurse	grudge	(*bash*)	(*spunge*)
since	purse	singe	casque	tongue
wince	badge	tinge	(*cask*)	(*tung*)
quince	edge	cringe	bosque	swerve
sconce	fledge	fringe	(*bosk,*	curve
dunce	pledge	twinge	gorge	false
farce	sledge	trudge	urge	once
copse	hedge	bilge	purge	(*wunse*)
corpse	ledge	bulge	surge	worse
manse	sedge	dinge	niche	(*wurse*

Vowel long. U prevents the silent E from softening the G

ba*the*	baste	plague	rogue	frize
la*the*	haste	scarce	brogue	(*frecze*)
sca*the*	paste	bli*the*	fugue	shire
swa*the*	taste	(w)ri*the*	clique	(*sheer*
ran*ie*	waste	scythe	(*cleek*)	or
change	*chaste*	force	pique	*shi-er*.)
stran*ge*	vague	borne	(*peek*)	

No. 69—LXIX.

Two Syllables. Accent on first.

Caution.—Do not say " gi-*unt*," " cli-*unt*," " base-*munt*," etc. ; but "gi-*ant*," " cli-*ent*," " base-*ment*," etc.

gi-ant	base-ment	whee-dle	li-vre
pli-ant	case-ment	i-dle	fe-male
tru-ant	pave-ment	bri-dle	do-tage
va-cant	pa-rent	ri-fle	va-cate
va-grant	la-tent	sti-fle	cli-mate
fla-grant	po-tent	tri-fle	pri-mate
fra-grant	fre-quent	o-gle	pi-rate
ty-rant	move-ment	bu-gle	pri-vate
cli-ent	a-ble	ma-ple	vi-brate
flu-ent	ca-ble	sta-ple	cu-rate
de-cent	fa-ble	stee-ple	fi-nite
re-cent	ga-ble	ti-tle	le-vite
tri-dent	ta-ble	bee-tle	safe-ty
pru-dent	sta-ble	sa-bre	nine-ty
stu-dent	fee-ble	fi-bre	sure-ty
a-gent	no-ble	a-cre	e-gress
re-gent	ru-ble	lu-cre	re-gress
co-gent	la-dle	me-tre	cy-press
si-lent	cra-dle	mi-tre	ba-sis
mo-ment	nee-dle	ni-tre	the-sis

No. 70—LXX.

Two Syllables. Accent on first.

cri.sis	a-pril	a-zure	pre-cept
pa-thos	a-corn	ba-bel	i-dol
fo-cus	ca.ret	cam-bric	i-dyl
bo-lus	brace-let	e-dict	mi-nor
mu'cus	sa-chem	e-pact	vi-and
wa-*ges*	dra-ma	e-qual	cli.max
ba.sin	a-*g*ed	e-ra	hy-dra
ma.son	sa-cred	de-ist	o-vert
ma-tron	ha-tred	de.ism	fo-rum
pa-tron	an-gel	de.mon	co-lon
a-pron	ha-ven	se-cret	re-script
(*a-purn*)	a-pex	te-nure	to-paz

Nine times ten make nine-ty.

A rose is fra-grant, that is, it has a grate-ful smell; but it is fa-ding.

Fe-males do much work with the nee-dle.

A ra-zor has a sharp edge. It is for sha-ving with.

We hang a large bell in a stee-ple, and it rings for church.

A watch is ver-y use-ful to tell the time. So is a clock.

The clock strikes twelve. It is time for us to be go-ing home.

A ca-ble is a strong thick rope for hold-ing fast a ship.

A purse-full of gold is the on-ly i-dol of the mi-ser.

An i-dle man is still in dan-ger of be-ing in want.

It is the sa-cred du-ty of a child to be kind to his pa-rents in old age.

A pi-rate is a bold, bad man. He spends his time in cha-sing ships, which he robs.

Let not sloth tri-umph o-ver you. The sloth-ful man is of no use in the world.

No. 71—LXXI.

Two Syllables.   Accent on Second.

Silent E preceded by a single consonant and a single vowel. The vowel in the accented syllable having its long or name sound.

de-face	su-preme	di-vine	in-voke	re-fute
ef-face	cam-phene*	o-blique†	pro-voke	com pute
dis-grace	se-rene	• de-sire	re-voke	dis-pute
cas-cade	ad-here	as-pire	con-sole	*I=E long*
pa-rade	co-here	in-spire	a-lone	an tique
de-grade	so vere	in-quire	de-throne	*(teek)*
un-safe	com-plete	re-quire	pro-rogue	cri-tique
as-suage	im-bibe	re-tire	a-dore	u-nique
en gage	ad-vice ¬	at-tire	be-fore	fa-tigue
in hale	en-tice	ad-mire	im-plore	*(teeg)*
re-gale	suf-fice	ad vise	ig-nore	in-trigue
de-fame	*(fize)*	chas-tise	de-pose	po-lice
in-sane	con-fide	de-vise	ex-pose	va-lise
pro-fane	de-ride	de-spise	im-pose	fás-cine
en-snare	de-cide	pre-cise	a-rose	ma rine
a-ware	di-vide	in-vite	de-note	ra-vine
be-ware	dis-like ¯	sur-prise	re-mote	sar-dine
e-rase	un-like	re quite	de-vote	ton-tine
de-bate	be-guile	de-spite	al-lude	ma-chine
e-late	de-file	po-lite	de-lude	Bra-zil
en-slave	com pile	re-vive	con-clude	cha-grin
o-paque	ex-ile	sur-vive	re-buke •	nan-kin
(pake)	eal-cine	a-live	mis-rule	*O=OO*
a-wake	com-bine	con-nive	as-sume	ap-provo
a maze	con-fine	de-prive	con-sume	re-move
ac-cede	re-pine	con-trive	pre-sume	dis-prove
con-cede	de-cline	as-size	de-mure •	re-prove
re-cede	sa-line	a-bode	as-sure	be-hove†
se-cure ¯	in-cline	ex-plode	*(shoor)*	*O=short U*
ex-treme	su-pine	cor-rode	re-fuse	a-bove

---

* Not *cam-phine*, at least not so in our dictionaries.
† Often pronounced *o-bleek*.
† Sometimes spelled *be-hoove*.

No. 72—LXXII.

Be-ware of u-sing pro-fane words.

Let us go and see the sol-diers pa-rade in the square.

A fas cine is a fag-ot or bun-dle of sticks.

You must a-wake at sun-rise to stud-y your les-son.

In-quire be-fore you de-cide.

Be po-lite to your com-rades (*kum*), and you will se-cure love in re-turn.

Some girls are fond of sty lish at-tire.

When you have made a prom-ise, see that you ad-here to it. You will be de-spised if you do not hold to your word.

To con-nive at the e-vil done by oth-ers is as bad as to as-sist in do-ing it.

An-tique gems and med-als are high-ly prized.

It is tire-some to go o ver the same les-sons time af-ter time; but you do it, to im prove.

We re-quire re pose af-ter la-bor; but we must not de-vote too much time to it.

We must not con-fine chil-dren to stud-y. A child's bod-y re-quires form-ing, as well as its mind.

Nan-kin is a buff cot-ton cloth, first made at Nan-kin, in Chi-na, whence its name.

It is un safe to fill a cam phene lamp while-it is burn-ing. The cam-phene in the can, as well as that in the lamp, may catch fire and ex-plode. Man-y per-sons have lost their lives in this man-ner.

" De-spise" is some times used for " dis-like." This is not a prop-er use of the word; and, be-sides, it is an ug-ly word when so used.

You must not de-face the desks or ta-bles at which you sit.

Bad ad-vice ru-ins man-y a man. Do not let it de-lude you.

Noth-ing (*nuth-ing*) en-slaves a man so much as e-vil hab-its.

We must try not to re-pine at ill for-tune, but rath-er strive to get the bet-ter of it.

Do not de-ride the mis takes of oth-ers: see that you do not fall in-to like mis-takes your-self.

No. 73.—LXXIII.

EE—E in *me ; OO* as in *LOO.*

CAUTION.—Do not drop the *R* in *door* and *floor,* and say *doe* and *floe.*

eel	peel	peer	food	gloom	roost
deed	reel	seer	good	groom	boo*th*
feed	creel	veer	hood	noon	smoo*th*
heed	steel	*cheer*	mood	soon	sooth
meed	wheel	queer	rood	spoon	soo*the*
need	deem	sheer	wood	swoon	troth
reed	seem	sneer	brood	coop	goose
seed	teem	steer	stood	whoop	loose
weed	keen	beet	hoof	loop	moose
bleed	seen	feet	loof	droop	noose
breed	green	meet	roof	scoop	ch*oose*
creed	queen	fleet	woof	sloop	groove
greed	sheen	greet	proof	stoop	foot
speed	screen	sheet	look	troop (*oo shorter*)
steed	spleen	sleet	cook	swoop	blood
beef	deep	sweet	hook	hoop	(*blud*)
reef	keep	street	look	boor	floo*d*
leek	peep	bee*ch*	nook	moor	(*flud*)
meek	weep	lee*ch*	rook	poor	door
reek	creep	spee*ch*	took	boot	(*dore*)
seek	sheep	teeth	brook	hoot	floor
week	sleep	flee*ce*	crook	moot	(*flore*)
cheek	steep	geese	boom	root	been
creek	sweep	cheese	loom	soot	(*bin*)
sleek	beer	sleeve	room	shoot	breech
feel	deer	breeze	bloom	boon	(*britch*)
heel	leer	freeze	broom	moon	

No. 74—LXXIV

Derivatives of two Syllables, ending in Y, -LESS, -NESS, -ING, -ED, -ER. Accent on the first Syllable.

need y	feed ing	feel er	look ing
reed y	heed ing	keep er	cool ing
weed y	need ing	weep er	bloom ing
greed y	bleed ing	sweep er	swoon ing
speed y	reek ing	mood y	droop ing
meek ly	seek ing	wood y	stoop ing
week ly	feel ing	room y	swoop ing
seem ly	deem ing	gloom y	foot ing
keen ly	seem ing	wool ly	shoot ing
queen ly	teem ing	cool ly	roost ing
deep ly	screen ing	poor ly	sooth ing
queer ly	keep ing	smooth ly	smooth ing
sweet ly	weep ing	loose ly	loos ing
need ful	creep ing	wood en	choos ing
cheer ful	sleep ing	wool len	hood ed
heed less	sweep ing	loos en	wood ed
need less	peer ing	fool ish	root ed
sleep less	veer ing	boor ish	soon er
peer less	cheer ing	roof less	coop er
cheer less	sneer ing	boot less	troop er
speech less	meet ing	foot less	poor er
meek ness	fleet ing	tooth less	roost er
keen ness	greet ing	good ness	smooth er
green ness	sheet ing	cool ness	oo==u in us
steep ness	freez ing	smooth ness	blood y
meet ness	heed ed	brood ing	blood less
fleet ness	need ed	roof ing	flood ed
sweet ness	greet ed	cook ing	flood gate

3

No. 75.—LXXV

Two Syllables. Accent on second.

			Three Syllables. Accent on first.
a–gree	con–gee	car–toon	ap-o–gee
a–sleep	de–cree	co–coon	fil-a–gree
be–see*ch*	de–gree	dra–goon	ju–bi–lee
be–tween	fu–see	fes–toon	ped-i–gree
can–teen	gran-dee	har–poon	per-i–gee
ca–reer	les–see	lam–poon	
com–peer	mar–quee	mon–soon	*Accent on third.*
dis–creet	·(*kee*)	pla–toon	ab–sen–tee
es–teem	o–gee	pol–troon	dev–o–tee
ex–ceed	set-tee	pon–toon	ep–o–pe
gen–teel.	trus–tee	rac–coon	leg-a–t
in–deed	a–loof	sa–loon	pat--en–t
pro–ceed	bal–loon	un–moor	ref-u–gee
suc–ceed	ba–boon	bam–boo	rep–ar–tee
mo–reen	bas–soon	hal loo	mac a roo
tu reen	be hoof	ta boo	pan ta loo
ve neer	buf foon	cuc koo	pic a roo

No. 76.—LXXVI.

One goose, two geese, three geese, and twelve state-ly
   swans with long, white necks, swim fine-ly on the
   smooth lake.

The fleece of the sheep is wool. We cut it off the
   sheep's back to make wool-len cloth.

The charge is put in-to some ri-fles at the breech.

It is shame-ful to have all that dirt on the floor
   Sweep it off quick-ly with a broom.

See that tri-fling tru-ant: he is there, roll-ing the
   hoop, when all the rest of his class are in school.

A groom takes care of a horse. He gives him his
   food in a man-ger, in the sta-ble.

Cheese is made from rich milk. Poor milk will not
   make good cheese.

The hoof of a horse or a po-ny is llke horn. It is
cut when the horse or the po-ny is shod.

Oh! Spring is a cheer-ful time Then, the grass
and the trees are green; and the brooks, which
the cold had fro-zen so hard, are loose from' i-cy
bonds once more.

Sponge is full of pores. You wash your slate with
a sponge; and it is a ve-ry nice thing to wash
the skin with.

There has been a gust. Look! the streets are
flood-ed.·

Swine feed on a-corns in the woods, and on the mast
which drops from the beech trees.

A leech sucks blood; and, when it is full, it will
loos-en its hold and drop off.

A coop er makes tubs of ce-dar wood. He keeps
the staves from get-ting loose by bind-ing them
with wood-en hoops.

Strive to be cheer-ful. You will find that no one
likes gloom-y looks.

Twelve o'clock is what we call noon.

If you are rich in this world's goods, think of those
who are poor and need-y, and give free-ly what
God has lent you; so shall your sleep be sweet.

You will nev-er suc-ceed in do-ing an-y thing worth
do-ing, un-less you la-bor.

The cuc-koo de-rives its name from its note.

A mar-quee is a tent made of strong can-vas, to keep
off the sun and the wet.

Win-ter is fast creep-ing up-on us. It will be cheer-
ing, in the cold win-ter time, to have plen-ty of
wood to make fires. If you are so hap-py, help
oth-ers who are not.

Think of the cheer-less a-bode of the poor,'who, in
this gloom-y win-ter, have lit-tle or no fire to
warm them, and pit-y them if you can do noth-
ing else.

If you can spell *meek*, you can soon spell *meek-er* and
meek-est, and *meek-ly*, and *meek-ness*.

Let me see if you can spell these words. You do
not think these hard words to spell, do you?

No. 77—LXXVII.

Words of two Syllables, and their derivatives of three,
accented on the second.

al ly	al li ance	a dorn	adorn ment
de fy	de fi ance	al lot	al lot ment
re ly	re li ance	a tone	a tone ment
ac quit	ac quit tance	at tach	at tach ment
ad mit	ad mit tance	bom bard	bom bard ment
re mit	re mit tance	de file	de file ment
as sist	as sist ance	de part	de part ment
re sist	re sist ance	de pend	de.pend ent
re pent	re pent ance	de port	de port ment
per form	per form ance	de scend	de scend ant
ac cord	ac cord ance	de tach	de tach ment
ab hor	ab hor rence	en camp	en camp ment
ad here	ad he rence	en dorse	en dorse ment
e merge	e mer gence	en force	en force ment
pre cede	pre ce dence	en gage	en gage ment
re cur	re cur rence	en hance	en hance ment
sub sist	sub sist ence	en large	en large ment
a gree	a gree ment	en tice	en tice ment
al lure	al lure ment	e quip	e quip ment
a maze	a maze ment	im pend	im pend ent
a base	a base ment	in duce	in duce ment
a but	a but ment	in form	in form ant
ad just	ad just ment	in vest	in vest ment

A be-gin-ner can-not be ex-pect-ed to go on un-less
he has as-sist-ance.

The re-pent-ance of an of-fend er does not can-cel
his of-fence. Re-morse will not a-tone for sin.

En-tice-ments to de-part from du-ty must be met
with firm re-sist-ance.

An ad-he-rence to the ex-act truth marks the con-
duct of all who have re-spect for them-selves.

Troops who en-ter a State with hos-tile purpose, are
in-va-ders. Let all who are able, take up arms to
drive them back.

He who is re-gard-less of the per-form-ance of his
du ty, must ex-pect, soon-er or la ter, to meet with
se-vere re-qui tal.

Of all that left the en-camp-ment to take part in the en-gage-ment, not more than one hun-dred sur-vived.

A dis til-ler makes strong drink from corn.

A large de-tach-ment was sent to share in the bom-bard-ment of the fort.

The word *a-muse-ment* is formed, from the word *a-muse* by add-ing *-ment* to it. If you can spell *a-muse*, it is not hard to spell *a muse-ment*.

All u-surp-ers are not op press-ors. Some of them have ruled wise-ly and well.

Which of us is not de-pend ent? Can a man ex-ist a lone? Not on-ly are we all de-pend ent on God, but no man can live, un-less he has the as-sist-ance of men like him self.

No. 78—LXXVIII.

re fine	re fine ment	de ny	de ni al
re tire	re tire ment	de spite	de spite ful
ob serve	ob serv ant	dis tress	dis tress ful
tran scend	tran scend ant	dis trust	dis trust ful
re spond	re spond ent	for get	for get ful
a bet	a bet tor	ne glect	ne glect ful
be gin	be gin ner	de part	de part ure
de sert	de sert er	in close	in clo sure
dis sent	dis sent er	a lert	a lert ness
dis til	dis til ler	ab rupt	ab rupt ness
im port	im port er	de mure	de mure ness
in spect	in spect or	ex act	ex act ness
in vade	in va der	for give	for give ness
in vent	in vent or	mi nute	mi nute ness
ob ject	ob ject or	pro fane	pro fane ness
of fend	of fend er	re gard	re gard less
op press	op press or	re miss	re miss ness
pro ject	pro ject or	re morse	re morse less
re cord	re cord er	a muse	a muse ment
re form	re form er	de spond	de spond ent
sur vive	sur vi vor*	dis close	dis clo sure
trans late	trans la tor	re quite	re qui tal
u surp	u surp er	re spect	re spect ful

* Sometimes spelled sur-vi-ver.

DIPHTHONGS AND TRIPHTHONGS.

A DIPH-THONG (*dip-thong*) is the union of two vowels forming one syllable.

A TRIPH-THONG (*trip-thong*) is the union of three vowels forming one syllable.

No. 79—LXXIX. IE.

Final *ie=i long.*			*ie=e long.*	
die,	died,	dies	fief	shield
hie,	hied,	hies	lief	fiend
lie,	lied,	lies	brief	priest
vie,	vied,	vies	grief	niece
ply,	plied,	plies	thief	piece
cry,	cried,	cries	chief	grieve
dry,	dried,	dries	bier	thieve
fry,	fried,	fries	pier	fierce
pry,	pried,	pries	tier	pierce
try,	tried,	tries	shriek	tierce
spy,	spied,	spies	field	siege
fly,		flies	wield	frieze
sty,		sties	yield	liege

Two Syllables. IE=E long.

Accent on first.		Accent on second.	
chief tain	field piece	a piece	a chieve
fierce ly	fierce ness	ag grieve	be lieve
griev ance	griev ous	re lieve	re prieve
priest ly	priest ess	re trieve	be lief
priest hood	priest craft	re lief	be siege
fron tier	thiev ish	Al giers	cash ier

IE=E long.

Three Syllables. Accent on third.

un be lief	brig a dier	cor de lier	cui ras sier
buc a nier*	can non ier*	fin an cier	(*kwe*)
car bi nier*	cav a lier	fu si lier	gon do lier
chan de lier	chev a lier	gren a dier	dis be lieve
(*shan*)	(*shev*)	bass re lief	dis be lief

* Sometimes spelled with *eer*; and *buc-a-nier* with two c's.

IE=E short.

friend	friend ly	friend ship
(*frend*)	friend less	span iel

IE=I short.

sieve	mis chief	ker chief	hand ker chief
(*siv*)	(*tshif*)	(*tshif*)	(*hang kur tshif*)

No. 80—LXXX.   OE.

Final OE=O long.*   *OE=E long.†*

doe, does	sloe, sloes	Oe ta	foe tus
foe, foes	throe, throes	phoe nix	an toe ci
hoe, hoed, hoes	fel loe		*OE=E short.‡*
roe, roes	mis tle toe	Oed i pus	Poec i le
toe, toes	(*miz zle toe*)		*OE=OO.*
floe, floes	*OE=U short.*	shoe	ca noe
	does		

No. 81—LXXXI.   UE.

UE=U LONG.

Two and three Syllables.

cue cues		*Accent on first.*		*Acct on sec'd.*
due dues	a gue	val ue		ac crue
hue hues	ar gue	vir tue		en sue
rue rued rues	con strue	(*ver*)		im bue
sue sued sues	is sue	Tues day		im brue
flue flues	(*ish*)	av e nue		en due
glue glued glues	tis sue	bar be cue		pur sue
clue clues	(*tish*)	res i due		sub due
blue	res cue	ret i nue		un true
true	stat ue	rev e nue		con tin ue

No. 82—LXXXII.

EU—EW—IEU—IEW—OEU—EAU.

EU=U long.   pleu ri sy   neu ral gi a

deuce	feud	feud a tory	Deu ter on o my
Eu rope	feud al	*IEU=U long.*	
neu ter	neu tral	lieu	pur lieu
eu lo gy	eu pho ny	a dieu	lieu ten ant‖

---

* In English words. † At the end of accented syllables in words derived from Latin. ‡ When followed by a consonant in the same syllable. ‖ Oftener *lev-ten-ant.*

EW=U long.

dew, dews	grew
hew, hewed, hewn, hews	he brew
mew, mewed, mews	ew er
new, news	pew ter
pew, pews	skew er
yew, yews	IEW=U long.
brew, brewed, brews	view viewed views
chew, chewed, chews	re view
clew, clews	in ter view
crew, crews	EW=O long.
stew, stewed, stews	sew
screw, screwed, screws	(so)
few, few-er, few-est	shew
blew	(sho)
flew	strew
slew	(stro)
drew	OEU=OO.
	ma nœu vre

EAU=U long.

beau ty	beau teous
beau ti ful	(bute yus)

EAU=O long.

beau	bu reau
beaus	flam beau
or	ron deau
beaux	port man teau

No. 83—LXXXIII. OA.

OA=O long.

goad	cloak	loan	oats	throat	coast
load	croak	moan	boat	coax	roast
road	coal	roam	coat	hoax	toast
toad	foal	groan	goat	oath	coach
woad	goal	soap	moat	loath	poach
oaf	shoal	oar	bloat	loathe	roach
loaf	foam	boar	float	board	broach
oak	loam	roar	gloat	hoard	coarse
soak	roam	soar	shoat	boast	hoarse

Two Syllables.

Accent on first.		Acct on sec'nd.	OA=AW
boat man	load star	a board	broad
be zoar	load stone	a float	groat
char coal	oak um	ap proach	a broad
co coa	oat meal	be moan	broad cloth
hoar hound	poach er	en croach	re proach
hoa ry	rail road	broad side	broad sword

A brew-er makes beer, and ale, and por-ter. These
are all made from malt, which is, it-self, made
from bar-ley.

The soot in the flue of a chim-ney some-times
catch-es fire, and then there is dan-ger of the
roof's be ing set on fire by the sparks.

When all the guns on one side of a ship of war are
fired at once, it is called a broad side.

Char-coal for fuel is made by pi-ling up logs two or
three feet long and three inch es thick, and cov-
er ing the pile with turf. A few holes are made
at the bot-tom of the pile, by which to ap-ply the
fire, and a few al so at the top, to let the smoke
e-scape. The wood thus cov-ered, is left to burn
for a week or two, and it is left to cool be-fore the
turf is re-moved.

The men on board a ves-sel, who work the ves-sel as
they are or-dered, are called the crew.

"Swear not at all." Some lads are fond of this sin-
ful prac-tice of swear-ing, for they think it is
man-ly. It is a sad thing that so man-y *men*
swear, as to make this hate-ful sin a sup-posed
proof of man hood. An oath must nev-er be ut
tered ex-cept when you are called up on as a wit-
ness in a tri-al.

The load-stone, or nat u-ral mag-net, is an ore of
i-ron (*i-urn*) met with in the mines of Swe-den and
Nor-way, in the isl-and (*i-land*) of El-ba, and else-
where. It has the prop-er-ty of at-tract-ing i-ron
or steel; and, when formed in-to a bar, hung by
its centre, and left free to move, it al-ways set-
tles al most North and South. It will give its
own prop-er-ties to a bar of steel by rub-bing.

No. 84—LXXXIV
AI—AY—EI—EY.

AI, AY, EI, EY=A LONG.

bay	play	laid	frail	plain	plaint
day	pray	maid	quail	slain	quaint
fay	slay	paid	snail	stain	plaice
gay	stay	raid	trail	train	raise
hay	spray	braid	maim	strain	praise
jay	tray	staid	claim	swain	maize
lay	stray	waif	fain	twain	veil
may	sway	bail	gain	bait	rein
nay	bey	fail	lain	gait	vein
pay	dey	hail	main	wait	skein
ray	hey	jail	pain	plait	feint
say	wey	mail	rain	trait	seine*
way	prey	nail	vain	strait	air
bray	they	pail	swain	faith	fair
clay	trey	rail	blain	faint	hair
flay	whey	sail	brain	paint	lair
dray	aid	tail	chain	saint	pair
fray	ail	wail	drain	taint	their

Derivatives, etc.   Two Syllables.   Accent in first.

dai ly	rail er	pray ing	strain ing	air pump
gai ly	sail or	slay ing	faint ing	cray on
main ly	tai lor	stray ing	aid ed	fail ure
vain ly	trai tor	sway ing	braid ed	rai sin
plain ly	may or	aid ing	paint ed	hail stone
fair ly	pray er†	ail ing	faint ed	bai liff
saint ly	wait er	aim ing	chair man	cai tiff
play ful	paint er	braid ing	lay man	plain tiff
gain ful	maid en	paint ing	claim ant	plain tive
pain ful	claim ant	fail ing	ail ment	chil blain
faith ful	lay ing	hail ing	rai ment	es say
aim less	pay ing	mail ing	way ward	cor sair
air less	say ing	wail ing	dai ry	por trait
brain less	bray ing	flail ing	fai ry	gain say
faith less	flay ing	quail ing	ey rie	way lay
gain er	fray ing	chain ing	frail ty	hei nous

* The dictionaries give the pronunciation *sene*.
† *Prayer*, a petition, is one syllable—*prair*.

Two Syllables. Accent on second.

al lay	pur vey	be wail	con strain	re main
ar ray	sur vey	de tail	de tain	re strain
af fray	dis may	en tail	dis dain	re straint
a stray	dis play	un veil	dis train	de claim
be tray	mis lay	a main	ex plain	de spair
de cay	por tray	at tain	main tain	af fair
de lay	as sail	com plain	(man tane)	un fair
de fray	a vail	com plaint	re frain	re pair
con vey	pre vail	con tain	re gain	a wait

AI, EI=I short.

CAUTION.—Do not say *cap-t'n, cer-t'n, cur-t'n*, etc.; but *cap-tin, cer-tin, cur-tin*, etc.

bar gain	cur tain	mur rain	quat rain	for feit
cap tain	chap lain	plan tain	quin tain	sur feit
cer tain	chief tain	quar tain	vil lain	coun ter feit

CAUTION.—Do not say *a-gain, a-gainst*, with the sound of *long A* in the second syllable, or *a-gin, a-ginst*, with the sound of *short I*; but *a-gen, a-genst*, with the sound of *short E*.

AI, EI=E short.   EI, EY=E long.

said	waist coat	ceil	con ceit	ei *ther*
saith	(*wes kut*)	seize	de ceit	nei *ther*
says	heif er	teil	con ceive	lei sure
a gain	*AI=A short.*	weird	de ceive	(*lee zhoor*)
a gainst	plaid	key	per ceive	in vei gle
wains cot	rail ler y	ceil ing	re ceive	

NOTE.—The termination pronounced *eeve*, when preceded by *c*, is spelled with *ei*; as, *con-ceive, de-ceive*: but when preceded by any other letter, it is spelled with *ie*; as, *grieve, re-lieve*. So also the derivatives; as, *con-ceit, de-ceit, grief, re-lief*.

No. 85—LXXXV

Do all you can to gain time; for if you are not a gain-er on time, time soon be a gain-er on you.

When the mail does not come dai ly, we wait for it some-times with keen-ly pain-ful feel-ings.

The life of a sail-or is sure ly a try-ing one. He may meet with foes in the shape of cor-sairs, or pi-rates, who lie in wait for rich pri zes; or storms may come, and winds may rave; and while his ship is fly ing swift ly in the gale, it may be dashed up-on a rock, when no eye can see, and no hand can help. Who has more need to pray to God than the poor sail-or?

When you have done say-ing your spell-ing, come, and we will look at the ne-groes hoe ing the corn.

A floe is a small sheet of ice. Floes are fre-quent in the north-ern bays and in lets; and there is much dan-ger to a ship in meet-ing with them.

When you are in the school-room, keep your place, and be si-lent. When you are called, come at once, and do not keep a class wait-ing for you.

A spray is a small branch of a tree. The white edge of a tall wave is named spray too. You see the same word is not al-ways used in the same sense.

A dai-ry is a place in which to keep milk, but-ter and cheese. It must be cool. Some dai-ries have a stream of wa-ter to cool them.

Hail is fro-zen rain. It falls in mass-es called hail-stones, which are some times ver-y large, and do much harm to the crops.

Some per-sons have chil-blains on their hands and feet in win ter. They are ver-y pain-ful.

When things do not go on as we wish, we must not com-plain, or give way to de-spair, but strive to meet all that be-falls us cheer-fully and hope-ful-ly.

> Ri-sing in yon-der sky of blue,
> While yet the grass is wet with dew,
> Blithe sings the lark his mat-in song
> In notes of glad-ness sweet and long.
> Like him, oh! hail the sun's first rays,
> And grate-ful sing thy Ma-ker's praise.

No. 86—LXXXVI. AU—AW.
AU, AW, like A in fall.

caw	saw	hawk	scrawl	drawn	maul
daw	taw	awl	sprawl	prawn	fault
haw	claw	bawl	dawn	spawn	vault
jaw	craw	brawl	fawn	daub	sauce
law	draw	yawl	lawn	gaud	pause
maw	flaw	crawl	pawn	laud	cause
paw	thaw	drawl	yawn	fraud	clause
raw	straw	shawl	brawn	haul	gauze

Derivatives, etc. Two Syllables. Accent on first.

law ful	drawl ing	vault ing	au spice	lau rel
law less	scrawl ing	paus ing	aus tral	mau gre
caw ing	sprawl ing	caus ing	au thor	pau per
paw ing	dawn ing	laud ed	aw ful	plau dit
saw ing	fawn ing	au burn	awk ward	sauce pan
draw ing	pawn ing	au dit	bau ble	sau cy
thaw ing	yawn ing	au ger	cau dle	saw yer
hawk ing	daub ing	aug ment	cau sey	saw dust
bawl ing	laud ing	au gur	caus tic	saw pit
brawl ing	haul ing	au gust	gau dy	taw dry
crawl ing	maul ing	au lic	haw thorn	taw ny

AU=A in far.

aunt	jaunt	haunch	gaunt let	laun dress
daunt	taunt	launch	jaun dice	saun ter
gaunt	vaunt	paunch	jaunt y	a skaunt*
haunt	flaunt	craunch	laun dry	a vaunt

AU=A long; gauge, gaug-er.
AU=O long; haut-boy (ho).

No. 87—LXXXVII. EA.
EA=E long as in ME.

pea	freak	cream	fear	neat	east
sea	sneak	dream	gear	peat	beast
tea	speak	gleam	hear	seat	feast
flea	squeak	scream	near	bleat	least

* Spelled also without the u.

plea	streak	stream	rear	*ch*eat	yeast
bead	deal	bean	sear	treat	ease
lead	heal	dean	*tear*	wheat	tease
mead	meal	lean	year	ea*ch*	please
read	peal	mean	shear	bea*ch*	cease
plead	seal	wean	clear	pea*ch*	lease
leaf	veal	clean	drear	tea*ch*	crease
sheaf	weal	glean	smear	rea*ch*	leave
beak	zeal	heap	spear	blea*ch*	weave
leak	steal	leap	eat	brea*ch*	heave
peak	beam	reap	beat	prea*ch*	cleave
weak	ream	*ch*eap	feat	leash	greave
bleak	seam	ear	heat	heath	brea*the*
creak	team	dear	meat	sheath	beard

Two Syllables. Accent on first.

bea con	crea ture	cas ter	mea sles	treat ment
bea dle	dea con	east ern	rea son	treat y
beak er	drea ry	fea ture	sea son	weak en
beat en	ea ger	hea *th*en	trea son	wea sel
bea ver	ea gle	mea gre	treat ise	clean ly

Two Syllables. Accent on second.

CAUTION.—Do not say *ap'pare* for *ap-pear*, *ar-rare* for *ar-rear*, etc. The sound is that of *ee*.

an neal	re veal	be smear	dis ease	re peat
ap peal	be speak	en dear	dis please	re treat
con ceal	de mean	ap pease	re lease	be reave
con geal	ap pear	de cease	de feat	im pea*ch*
re peal	ar rear	de crease	en treat	be nea*th*

EA=E short as in met.

dead	dread	deaf	breath	earl	dearth
head	spread	threat	wealth	pearl	heard
lead	tread	sweat	health	realm	breast
read	thread	meant	stealth	earn	sear*ch*
bread	stead	death	earth	yearn	cleanse

Two Syllables. Accent on first.

clean ly	feath er	jeal ous (us)	treas ure (zh
ear ly	leath er	zeal ous (us)	break fast
heav y	weath er	peas ant	ear nest
read y	heav en	pheas ant	earl dom
stead y	leav en	pleas ant	mead ow
stealth y	threat en	meas ure (zh)	zeal ot
wealth y	weap on	pleas ure (zh)	

Accent on second.

a head	be stead	re hearse
be head	in stead	re search

EA=A long. | EA=A in far.

break	steak	pear	wear	heart	hearth
great	bear	tear	swear	heart y	heark en

No. 88—LXXXVIII.

Wheat ri-pens in June. It is pleas-ant to see the
reap ers cut-ting it. They be gin al most at the
dawn of day, and work hard till sun-set. When
the grain is well dried, it is ta ken to the mill, and
there the mil ler grinds it to make bread for us
to eat.

Let us go to the mead ow, and look at the hay-
ma-kers. Some are cut-ting the grass with a long
scythe; while some are spread-ing it to the sun.
When dry, the grass is called hay. It is then
built up in-to hay-stacks and left in the field, or
hauled home and stored in the barn to feed the
cat-tle du-ring the bleak weath-er of win ter, when
no green food is to be had.

It be-gins to threat-en rain. The vault of heav-en
is dark-en ing. Do you not hear the thun-der?
We shall have a heav y gust be-fore we can reach
home. Let us hur ry to some shel-ter where we
can stay till it clears—

"The haw-thorn whi-tens; and the groves
Put forth their buds, un-fold-ing by de-grees,
Till the whole leaf-y for-est stands dis-played;"

For, it is Spring,—Spring, of all the sea sons of the year most cheer ful. Then, the earth wakes from the drea ry sleep of win ter, and be gins to clothe her-self in her love ly robe of green. "The birds sing, con-cealed." "The moun tains lift their green heads to the sky." The brook leaps mer-ri-ly o ver its peb bly chan-nel, and "chat ters—chat ters, as it flows to join the brim ming riv-er." E ven "re vi ving sick-ness lifts his lan guid head." All na-ture smiles, and sends up a song of praise to the great Cre-a-tor.

Feath ers are the cloth-ing of birds. Some of them are of the most gau-dy and va ried col ors, as those of the par-rot; while oth-ers are of very so-ber col ors, as those of the com mon barn-yard fowl. The feath ers are fixed in the skin by a quill. In the wing of the larg er birds, these quills are of great size; and those of the goose's wing are made in-to pens to write with.

Eas ter comes in March or A-pril, at the end of the sea-son of Lent.

Peat is a soft spong y earth. In some pla ces it is cut in-to small squares, and dried in the sun to be used as fu el. It is put up in stacks which are thatched to keep off the rain.

The fur of the bea ver is used in ma king hats.

A ream of pa-per con tains twen-ty quires.

> Hap-py the man, whose wish and care,
> A few pa-ter-nal a-cres bound,
> Con-tent to breathe his na-tive air
> In his own ground.
>
> Whose herds with milk, whose fields with bread,
> Whose flocks sup-ply him with at-tire,
> Whose trees in sum-mer yield him shade,
> In win-ter fire.

The pheas-ant is a na-tive of A-si-a (A-zhe-a); so al-so is the pea-cock, and so are our com-mon fowl.

Moth-er-of-pearl is the in-ner coat-ing of the shell to which pearls ad-here.

It is pleas ant to rise ear-ly in sum-mer, and take a stroll o-ver the fields be-fore break-fast.

No. 89—LXXXIX: OU—OW.

OU, OW=Ah and OO combined.

cow	scowl	proud	shout	*ch*ouse	mount
how	down	shroud	snout	grouse	couc*h*
now	gown	foul	spout	bound	crouc*h*
vow	town	sour	trout	found	slouc*h*
brow	brown	flour	stout	hound	mouth
prow	crown	scour	sprout	mound	south
crowd	drown	bout	gou*g*e	pound	ounce
owl	browse	gout	douse	round	bounce
cowl	blowze	pout	house	sound	pounce
fowl	our	rout	mouse	*wound*	flounce
howl	out	clout	rouse	ground	trounce
growl	oust	flout	souse	count	route
prowl	cloud	scout	spouse	fount	loun*g*e

Two Syllables.

CAUTION.—Be careful not to drop the *e*, in such words as *tow-el, cow-er*, etc.

Accent on first.

dow ry	show er	coun ty	out let
drow sy	pow der	foun dry	out line
row el	owl et	coun sel	out ra*g*e
tow el	prow ess	ground sel	out ward
vow el	cow ard	spous al	south ward
trow el	dow las	coun *c*il	thous and
cow er	down cast	coun ter	foun tain
dow er	down fall	foun der	*(tin)*
low er	down ward	floun der	moun tain
pow er	town clerk	trou sers	*(tin)*
tow er	towns man	count ess	found ling
flow er	boun ty	mouth ful	ground plot

Accent· on second.

a vow	with out	a round	e spouse
al low	ac count	as tound	an nounce
en dow	a mount	ex pound	de nounce
re nown	dis count	pro found	re nounce
de vour	re count	re bound	pro nounce
a loud	re mount	re sound	a vouch
a bout	sur mount	sur round	vouch safe
de vout	a bound	ca rouse	sou chong*

OU and OW=O long as in No.

owe	blow	show	mown	growth	mourn
bow	flow	snow	sown	soul	court
low	glow	stow	flown	four	poult
mow	slow	strow	grown	pour† ·	source
row	crow	throw	shown	mould	course
sow	grow	bowl	strown	gourd	fourth
tow	trow	own	thrown	bourn	moult

Two Syllables. Accent on first.

CAUTIONS.—Avoid pronouncing the final *ow* like *er;* as, *win-der* for *win-dow*, *wid-der* for *wid-ow*.

Avoid accenting *towards* on the second syllable—*to-wards'*

own er	snow drop	hal low	hol low	mor row
low er ·	mead ow	sal low	ar row	sor row
bow yer	(med)	tal low	bar row	whit low
mould er	shad ow	shal low	far row	poul tice
tow ards	el bow	swal low	har row	· poul try
bow man	win dow	bel low	mar row	four fold
bow sprit	win now	fel low	nar row	four teen
snow ball	wil low	fol low	spar row	four score

---

* The more common pronunciation of this word is *soo-shong.*
† The pronunciation rhyming with *our* is seldom, if ever, heard; and still less frequently that rhyming with *your.*

$OU = U$ short as in US.

touch	coup let	doub let	nour ish
young	cour age	trou ble	south ern
scourge	cous in	jour nal	touch stone
joust	cou ple	jour ney	house wife
coun try	dou ble	flour ish	(huz wif)

$OU = OO$.

bouse	tour	youth	a mour
croup	you	cou(l)d	con tour
group	your	wou(l)d	sur tout
soup	*wound*	shou(l)d	un couth

No. 90—XC. OI—OY

OI, OY = AW and EE combined.

CAUTION.—Avoid the vulgarism of pronouncing *OI* like the long *I*; as, *ile* for *oil*, *jine* for *join*, *pint* for *point*.

boy	coil	void	foist	poise
coy	foil	coin	hoist	quoit
joy	soil	join	joist	(*koit*)
toy	toil	loin	moist	choir
cloy	broil	groin	voice	(*quire*)
oil	spoil	joint	choice	buoy
boil	coif	point	noise	(*boo oy*)

Two Syllables.

Accent on first.		Accent on second.		
boy ish	joint ure	al loy	a droit	re join
boy hood	broid er	an noy	ex ploit	re joice
joy ful	poi. son	de coy	de spoil	a noint
coy ly	oint ment	de stroy	em broil	ap point
toy shop	clois ter	en joy	re coil	bour geois
voy age	oys ter	em ploy	ad join	(*bur joice*)
loy al	moist ure	sa voy	con join	pur loin
roy al	in voice	a void	dis join	a roint
coin age	con voy	de void	en join	un coil

No. 91—XCI.   UI.

UI=OO, and U long.		*UI=I long.*	
bruit	juice	buy	guy
fruit	suit	guide	guise
bruise	pur suit	(*gyide*)	(*gyize*)
cruise	re cruit	guile	dis guise
sluice	nui sance	(*gyile*)	(*diz gyize*)

UI=I short as in Pin.			*UI=WE.*
build	bis cuit	lan guish	suite
guild	cir cuit	san guine	(*sweet*)
built	con duit	an guish	cui rass
guilt	lan guid	lin guist	(*kwe*)
guin ea	(*lang gwid*)	guil lo tine	pur sui vant

No 92—XCII.   EO.

EO=E long.	*EO=AW*	*EO=E short.*
peo ple	George	Leon ard
EO=O long.	Geor gie	leop ard
yeo man	Geor gi a	jeop ard
yeo man ry		jeop ard y

No. 93—XCIII.   OUS.

Two Syllables.   Accent on first.

ous=us.			*ious and eous =yus.*
fa mous	mu cous	joy ous	bil ious
gle bous	cal lous	mon strous	beau teous
fi brous	cum brous	ner vous	du teous
vi nous	fun gous	pom pous	cour teous
glo bous	gib bous	schir rous	(*kur*)
no dous	jeal ous	vis cous	boun teous
po rous	zeal ous	won drous	ri(gh)t eous

geous=jus ; cious, scious, tious, scous=shus ;
xious=k-shus.

gor geous	spe cious	cau tious
gra cious	vi cious	fac tious
lus cious	*(vish us)*	nau seous
pre cious	con scious	anx ious
(presh us)	cap tious	nox ious

Three Syllables. Accent on first.
ous=us.

scan da lous	rav en ous	bois ter ous
li bel lous	res in ous	tim o rous
per il ous	glut ton ous	cred u lous
in fa mous	poi son ous	em u lous
blas phe mous	vil lain ous	fab u lous
post (h)u mous	dan ger ous	scrof u lous
ven om ous	dex ter ous	sul phu rous
lu mi nous	gen er ous	ven tu rous
glu ti nous	on er ous	mis chiev ous
mu ti nous	pon der ous	*(tshiv)*
ru in ous	pros per ous	quer u lous

ious, eous=ee-us.

du bi ous	en vi ous	pit e ous
o di ous	ob vi ous	vit re ous
stu di ous	per vi ous	*uous=u-us*
co pi ous	pre vi ous	ar du ous
cu ri ous	a que ous	con gru ous
glo ri ous	fer re ous	stren u ous
se ri ous	hid e ous	sump tu ous
spu ri ous	ig ne ous	unc tu ous
va ri ous	lac te ous	vir tu ous
de vi ous	o chre ous	*(ver)*

Accent on second.

de co rous	so no rous

Accent on second.

geous, gious=jus ; ceous, cious, tious=shus ;
xious=k-shus.

I preeeding the terminations -*cious*, -*tious*, has its
short sound, and combines with the sound *sh*,
making -*icious*, -*itious*=*ish-us*.

cour a geous	ca pa cious	ju di cious
(*kur*)	fal la cious	ma li cious
out ra geous	lo qua cious	of fi cious
um bra geous	ra pa cious	am bi tious
con ta gious	sa ga cious	fac ti tious
li ti gious	te na cious	fic ti tious
re li gious	in nox ious	nu tri tious
cre ta ceous	ob nox ious	fa ce tious
pre da ceous	aus pi cious	a tro cious
tes ta ceous -	ca pri cious	fe ro cious
au da cious	de li cious	in fec tious

No. 94—XCIV

The snow-drop is one of the ear-li-est spring flow-
ers. It some times makes its ap-pear-ance when
the ground is cov ered with snow, whence prob-a-
bly its name.

What a pure white is the col-or of the snow! It
falls in flakes ; and, in cold cli-mates re-mains on
the ground for a long time. When melt-ed, it is
wa-ter; but, if you fill a ves sel with snow, and
let it dis solve, the ves-sel will not be filled by the
wa ter. The bulk of new fall-en snow is ten or
or twelve times great-er than the bulk of the wa-
ter ob-tained by melt-ing it.

What sport the boys and girls in cold coun-tries
have in win-ter, in throw-ing snow balls at each
oth-er, and roll-ing each oth-er in the snow !

Sou-chong is the kind of black tea most com-mon ly
im-port ed in-to this coun-try from Chi-na where
it grows. There are two oth-er kinds of black
tea, be-sides three kinds of green tea. Tea is the

leaves of the tea plant dried on i-ron (*i-urn*) plates.
Sev er-al tri-als have been made to pro-duce tea in
oth-er coun-tries than Chi-na, but with-out suc-cess.
Su gar is pro-duced in the West In-di-es, and in our
own South-ern States. It is made from the juice
of the su-gar cane which is pressed out by crush
ing the cane in a mill. This juice, after boil ing
and oth er treat-ment, yields brown su-gar, mo-
lass-es, white or loaf sugar, and su-gar can-dy.
Next to their pa-rents, chil-dren have rea-son to be
most grate-ful to their teach-ers, who la bour faith-
ful-ly to in-struct them, so that, when they grow
up to be men and wo men (*wim-men*), they may be
good men and wo-men, and use-ful to them-selves
and oth-ers.
Tal-low is the melt-ed and strained su-et of the ox
and sheep. . It is made in to can-dles and soap, be
sides be-ing used in dress-ing leath-er, and in va-
ri ous proc-ess es in the arts.
A crown is the sym-bol of roy-al-ty, placed on the
head of a king or queen on com-ing to the throne.
A crown is al-so a Brit-ish coin or piece of mon-
ey, in val-ue a lit-tle more than a dol-lar.
The word *b-u-o-y* some per-sons find hard to pronounce. The *u* is like *oo ;* so, we pro-nounce the
word, *boo-oy*, or *bwoy*, but not, as we some-times
hear it, *boo-e*, or *bwee*.

O Thou, to whom all crea-tures bow
　Within this earth-ly frame,
In all the world how great art Thou,
　How glo-ri ous is Thy name!

In Heaven Thy won-drous acts are sung,
　Nor ful-ly reck-oned there :
And yet Thou mak'st the in-fant tongue
　Thy bound-less praise de-clare.

In the be-gin-ning of this cen-tu-ry there was not a
steam-boat or a rail-road in the world. Now,
steam-boats nav-i-gate all wa-ters, and rail-roads
trav-erse near-ly ev-er-y coun-try ; and now, we
can trav-el by land or by sea, a dis-tance in a few
hours, which, six-ty years a-go, would have required as man-y days.

VARIABLE CONSONANT SOUNDS.*

C is *soft*, that is, it sounds like *S*, before *E*, *I*, and *Y* In all other situations it is *hard*, that is, it sounds like *K*.

The following list contains examples of both sounds. Let the learner point them out.

No. 95—XCV   C.

cem ent	cit ron	cen o taph	sac ra ment†
cen sure	civ ic	cic a trice	sic ci ty
cen sus	cy cle	(*tris*)	cel i ba cy
cen to	cy cloid	cic a trize	cem e ter y
ce rate	cym bal	cin na mon	cen te na ry
ces tus `	cyn ic	cir cum flex	cer e mon y
cin der	cy press	cir cum stance	ce leb ri ty
cir cus	flac cid	cit a del	cen tu rion
cit rine	cel e brate	cit i zen	ce ru le an
(*rin*)	cel er y	civ il ize	cir cum fer ence

No. 96—XCVl.   G.

G is generally soft, that is it sounds like *J*, before *E*, *I*, and *Y*. In all other situations it is hard, that is it sounds as in *gun*.

gel id	gip sy	gran deur	gem i ni
ge nus	gal lows	sug gest‡	gen e sis
gib bet ⸱	(*lus*)	gal ax y	goose ber ry
gin ger	gos pel	gal ler y	ges tic u late
gin seng	glob ule	gar ru lous	ex ag ger ate.

---

* The preceding pages necessarily contain many examples of these variable sounds, some of which may possibly be inadvertently repeated here.

† Not *sa-cra-ment*.

‡ Both *G*'s are soft in *exaggerate*; only the last in *sug-gest*, though we sometimes hear the pronunciation *sud-jest*.

In the following words, *G* is hard before *E* and *I*.

gear	gilt	dag ger	fin ger	big gin
geck	gimp	stag ger	lin ger	pig gin
geese	gird	swag ger	gib ber	nog gin
get	girl	trig ger	gib bous	drug gist
gift	girt	ti ger	gid dy	be gin'
gig	girth	an ger	gim let	for give'
gild	give	ea ger	gir dle	mis give'
gill	gew gaw	au ger	giz zard	for get'

G is also hard in the terminations *-ged, -ger, -gy, -ging, -gish,* when annexed to words ending in *G.*

snag	snag ged	dog	dog ged	fog	fog gy
crag	crag ged	dig	dig ger	crag	crag gy
rag	rag ged	rig	rig ger	rig	rig ging
scrag	scrag ged	bog	bog gy	wag	wag gish

No. 97—XCVII. CH.

CH has three sounds. 1. It is soft, like *tsh,* in English words; as *church, chide.* 2. It is hard, like *K,* in words derived from the ancient languages; as *chord, scheme.* 3. It sounds like *SH,* in words derived from French, and in the terminations *-lch, -nch, -tch ;* as *chaise, filch, bench, witch.*

CH soft=TSH.

chal dron	cher ub	chas ti ty
(*chawl*)	ur chin	chas tise ment
chal ice	cham pi on	cher u bim
chap let	chan ti cleer	choc o late

CH hard=K.

ache	sched ule	chrys o lite
chasm	schol ar	eu cha rist
chyle	schoon er	hi e rarch
scheme	o chre	mon ar chy
an arch	an ar chy	pen ta teuch
cho ral	an cho ret	a nach' ro nism
chris tian	cat e chism	cha lyb' e ate
chris(t) mas	chem i cal	cha me' le on
ep och	chol er a	chro nom' e ter
mon arch	chor is ter	mo narch' i cal
stom ach	chron o gram	pa ro' chi al

4

ARCH.

Arch, when it is a prefix to English words, has *ch* soft; as *arch-deacon;* but when it forms a part of a word derived from Greek, it has *ch* hard; as *arch-i-tect*.

The prefix Arch.	*Arch in Greek words.*
arch duke	ar chives
arch wise	ar chi tect
arch dea con	'ar che type
arch prel ate	ar chi trave
arch bish op	ar cha ism
arch duch ess	arch an' gel
arch pres by ter	ar chai ol' o gy
arch bish op rick	ar chi o pis' co pate
arch dea con ry	ar chi di ac' o nate

No. 98—XCVIII.

In the following reading lesson, let the learner point out C, G, or CH, soft or hard, wherever any of them occurs, and give the reason of the sound.

Ge-og-ra-phy can-not be well stud-ied with-out a map.

It is grate-ful to the feel-ings to see a cem-e-ter-y well ta-ken care of.

A cen-tu-ri-on in the Ro-man ar-my com-mand-ed a hun-dred men. He was e-qual in rank to a cap-tain in our ar-mies.

The sky, when free from clouds, is of a ce-ru-le-an hue.

The glob-ules of dew glit-ter in the rays of the ri-sing sun.

The cin-ders of bi-tu-mi-nous coal make a ver-y hot fire.

A speak-er should not ges-tic-u-late too much.

The skin of the cham-ois (*sham-oy'*) fur-nish-es leath-er of which gloves are made.

Chess is a ver-y dif-fi-cult game to play well.

A car-pen-ter fre-quent-ly adds to his oc-cu-pa-tion that of an ar-chi-tect.

A news-pa-per is a chron-i-cle of pass-ing e-vents.

A-rith-me-tic is the low-est de-part-ment of math-e-mat-ics.

The cha-me-le-on clings to the branch-es of trees, and there waits to catch the in-sects on which it lives. It is said to change its col or at pleas-ure.

Choc-o-late is made from the ker-nel of the co-coa-nut.

Al-most ev-er-y art has tech-ni cal terms pe-cu-li-ar to it-self.

The first five books of the Old Tes-ta-ment are called the Pen-ta-teuch.

The moon be-tween the half moon and the full moon is said to be gib-bous.

The gip-sies are a wan-der-ing race of peo-ple who in-fest the old world; ro-ving a-bout with-out reg-u-lar em-ploy-ment, and sup-port-ing them-selves by theft, rob-ber-y, and for-tune-tell-ing.

A Geor-gic is a po-em on ru-ral af-fairs. Vir-gil com-posed four books of Geor-gics.

A cat-e-chism is a se-ri-es (*se-re-eze*) of ques-tions and an-swers on an-y sub ject.

Drugs and min-er-al wa-ters con-tain-ing i-ron are called *cha-lyb-e-ates.*

A *chro-nom-e-ter* is a watch of pe-cu-liar con-struc-tion and great per-fec-tion of work-man-ship; used at sea, and some-times on rail-roads, and wher-ev-er it is nec-es-sary to meas-ure time with ex-treme ac-cu-ra-cy.

The word "chas-tise" is ac-cent-ed on the sec-ond syl-la-ble; but its de-riv-a-tive "chas-tise-ment" is ac-cent-ed on the first; and be-sides, the *I* of the prim-i-tive is short-ened in the de-riv-a-tive. You must learn to ob-serve such things.

The word "chor-is-ter" is some-times pro-nounced as if spelled "quir-is-ter," prob-a-bly be-cause its prim-i-tive "choir" is pro-nounced "quire."

Do not for-get that ev-er-y read-ing les-son is to be a spell-ing les-son. This is a dif-fi-cult les-son, and it should be read sev-er-al times.

No. 99—XCIX. S.

S has two sounds, one sharp and hissing as in *us, thus;* the other flat like z, as in *his, is.**

In the following words, and their derivatives, *dis=diz.* Other words beginning with this prefix have the *S* sharp.

Dis = Diz.

dis arm	dis grace	dis mask	dis (h)on est
dis band	dis guise	dis may	dis (h)on or
dis bark	dis gust	dis miss	dis loy al
dis burse	dis join	dis mount	dis man tle
dis cern	dis junct	dis solve	dis mem ber
(*diz zern*)	dis like	dis vouch	dis mor(t) gage
dis dain	dis lim(b)	dis a ble	dis or der
dis ease	dis lodge	dis as ter	dis val ue
dis gorge	dis mal	dis bur den	dis in ter est ed

Words in *-ase, -ese, -ise, -ose, -use,†* have the *S* sharp; except *wise, guise, these,* and *those.*

a base	pre cise	mor bose	mo rose	re cluse
o bese	glo bose	jo cose	pro fuse	ob struse
con cise	ver bose	ru gose	dif fuse	ob tuse

Words in *-sive* have the *S* sharp.

per sua sive	de ri sive	con clu sive	pre lu sive
dis sua sive	a bu sive	ex clu sive	il lu sive
ad he sive	dif fu sive	e lu sive	a mu sive
co he sive	in fu sive	de lu sive	in tru sive
de ci sive‡	in ch sive	al lu sive	ob tru sive

Words in *-sary* and *-sory,* except *ro-sa-ry,* have the *S* sharp.

dis pen sa ry	com pul so ry	re spon so ry
per sua so ry	in cen so ry	dis cur so ry
in ci so ry	com pen so ry	e lu so ry
de ri so ry	sus pen so ry	il lu so ry

In the termination *-esce,* the *sc* is pronounced as *ss.*

ac qui esce	co a lesce	ef fer vesce	ev a nesce

---

* It would be impossible here to give rules for the sounds of *S.* Only a few important lists are given, all containing words liable to mis-pronunciation.

† Generally *adjectives* or *nouns.* *Verbs* of these endings have the *S* flat; *a-base,* however, is an exception.

‡ Not *de-ciz-ive.*

No. 100—C. *X*

X has two sounds; one sharp, like *ks*, as in *ex-cuse*, the other flat, like gz, as in *ex-ist*.

It has almost always the sharp sound *ks*. The flat sound *gz* is found only in the words

lux u ri ant	anx i e ty
lux u ri ate	ex em pla ry
lux u ri ous	

and in the prefix *ex* when followed by an accented syllable beginning with a vowel or *h*.

Ex=Egz.

CAUTION.—*H* following *ex* must not be silent. Do not say *ex-ort*, but *ex-hort*, aspirating the *H*.

Accent on second Syllable.

ex act	ex ist	ex ot ic	ex em pli fy
ex alt	ex ult	ex us tion	ex ig u ous
ex empt	ex am ine	ex hil a rate	ex on er ate
ex ert	ex am ple	ex an i mate	ex or bi tant
ex hale	ex an tiate	ex as per ate	ex os se ous
ex haust	ex em plar	ex ec u tive	ex u ber ant
ex hort	ex e sion	ex ec u tor	ex u vi ae
ex ile	ex hib it	ex eo u trix	ex or di um

When *X* begins a word, it sounds like *z*, as in *Xerx-es.*

No. 101—CI. *GH.*

Gh in the beginning of a word or syllable drops the *H*; as in *ghost, ghast-ly, a-ghast, gher-kin.*

At the end of words, when not silent

GH=F.

laugh	trough	slough	e nough
(*laff*)	(*troff*).	(*sluff*)	(*e nuff*)
draught	clough	rough	*GH=K.*
(*draft*)	(*kloff*)	(*ruff*)	hough
cough	chough	tough	(*hock*)
(*koff*)	(*chuff*)	(*tuff*)	lough
			(*lock*)

No. 102—CII. N.

N has the sound of *ng* when it precedes *k* or *x* in the same syllable, as *link, minx;* or, when it ends an accented syllable followed by *g hard, k* or *q;* as *an-gle, an-kle, ban-quet,* pronounced *an-gl, an-kl, bang-kwet.*

N=NG.

an ger	con quest	min gle	strong est
bank er	an gle	sin gle	young est
fin ger	dan gle	tin gle	lar ynx
lin ger	fan gle	shin gle	syr inx
long er	jan gle	tin kle	pha lanx
hun ger	man gle	sprin kle	dis tinct'
mon ger	tan gle	bun gle	ex tinct'
strong er	(w)ran gle	jun gle	de lin' quent
young er	span gle	mon grel	dis tin' guish
clan gor	stran gle	tran quil	ex tin' guish
lan guor	in gle	con cord	re lin' quish
con quer	jin gle	long est	e lon' gate

No. 103—CIII. TH and PH.

Th has two sounds; one sharp, as in *thin, think;* the other flat, as in *this, these.*

Th in words derived from Greek, and at the beginning or end of English words, is sharp, as *throng, bath, the-sis, the-a-tre.*

Th sharp.

thank	thieve	sheath	pa thos
thatch	thrum	tooth	e ther
thaw	thrust	teeth	eth ics
theft	thwart	truth	meth od
theme	thrush	health	the a tre
thick	bath	wealth	the o ry
thief	birth	stealth	the o rist
thin	death	worth	ap a thy
thing	breath	youth	sym pa thy
think	cloth	myth	leth ar gy
third	doth	bis muth	a the ist
thirst	earth	ze nith	am e thyst
thong	faith	the ism	ep i thet

thorn	bath	the sis	or tho dox
thrall	lath	thim ble	cath o. lic
thrash	loth	thir teen	pleth o ric
thread	moth	thir ty	syn the sis
threat	month	thresh old	mis an thrope
three	mouth	thurs day	hy a cinth
thrice	oath	thral dom	am a ranth
thrive	path	au thor	lab y rinth
throng	quoth	ba-thos	thir ti eth

The following English words have the initial and final *th* flat.

this	thee	then	those	thine
that	their	thence	thou	seeth
than	them	these	thus	booth
the	there	they	thy	smooth

Th, in the middle of pure English words, is also flat.

fath er	hea then	smoth er	neth er
gath er	hith er	broth er	far thing
lath er	thith er	ei ther	north ern
rath er	with er	nei ther	south ern
heath er	whith er	breth ren	worth y
feath er	oth er	fath om	weth er
leath er	moth er	far ther	to geth er

Silent E added to words ending in *th* sharp, renders the *th* flat; as it always is in the termination *-the*, except in *withe*, which has *th* sharp.

bath	bathe	loath	loathe		blithe
lath	lathe	cloth	clothe		tithe
swath	swathe	sheath	sheathe		scythe
breath	breathe	sooth	soothe		writhe

S added also frequently softens the final *th*.

bath	baths	path	paths	mouth mouths	cloth	cloths
lath	laths	oath	oaths	truth truths	youth	youths

With.

With and its compounds in which *with* is placed first, have the *th* flat.

with	with al	with hold
with in	with draw	here with al
with out	with stand	there with al

But the compounds in which *with* comes last have the *th* sharp; as

fórth with   here with   there with   where with

PH.

Ph has the sound of *F;* except in *neph-ew* and *Ste-phen*, in which it sounds like *V*

phan tom	phar ma cy	phys i cal	phre net' ic
phi al	phil o mel'	phi lip' pic	al pha bet
phil ter	phil o math	phi lis' tine	cen o taph
phys ics	phos pho rus	phleg mat' ic	por phy ry
phoe nix	pho no type	phlo gis' ton	aph o rism
pha e ton	pho to graph	pho net' ic	eph o rus

No. 104.—CIV

It is dis-grace-ful for a man to be dis-loy-al to his coun-try.

A per-son of mo-rose dis-po-si-tion makes him-self un-hap-py, and dis-gusts those a-round him.

We must not ex-pect to be en-tire-ly ex-empt from suf-fer-ing. Af-flic-tion at some time and in some shape is the lot of hu-man-i-ty.

Let your con-duct be ex-em-pla-ry, that is, cal-cu-la-ted to make you an ex-em-plar to oth-ers.

It is hard to con-quer a hab-it; there-fore we must take care not to ac-quire bad ones.

A cough is fre-quent-ly the symp-tom of se-ri-ous dis-ease.

Do not laugh at the mis-takes of your school-mates, but rath-er help them to cor-rect them.

On the coast of Ire-land an arm of the sea is called a lough.

Man-y poor peo-ple who live in large cit-ies can hard-ly pro cure e-nough to sat-is-fy hun-ger.

A withe is made of some tough wood, to bind poles to-geth-er with, to make scaf-fold-ing, and for oth-er pur-po-ses which re-quire a strong band.

The depth of wa-ter is meas-ured in fath-oms. A fath-om is two yards or six feet.

The most north-ern and the most south-ern points of the earth are ealled the poles. Nei-ther of them has ev-er been reached by man.

The in-hab-it-ants of the parts of the earth whieh are un-der the e-qua-tor, have the sun ex-act-ly in their ze-nith or the point di-rect-ly o-ver-head, on the twen-ti-eth of March, and the twenty-third of Sep-tem-ber. We nev-er have the sun in our ze-nith.

The Jew-ish Sab-bath is Sat-ur-day, the last day of the week. The Chris-tian Sab-bath is Sun-day, the first day of the week.

Be-neath a rough ex-te-ri-or we some-times find kind and ten-der feel-ings.

Ath-ens was for-mer-ly the most re-fined cit-y in Eu-rope.

> Oh, 'tis a love ly thing for youth
> To wa(l)k be-times in Wis-dom's way;
> To fear a lie, to speak the truth,
> That we may trust to all they say.

SILENT LETTERS.

No. 105.—CV

1. *B* is silent when it follows *m* or precedes *t* in the same syllable; as *lamb, debt;* also in the word *sub-tle.* EXCEPTIONS.—In *rhomb, ac-cumb,* and *suc-cumb,* the *b* is distinctly pronounced.

2. *G* is silent before *m* or *n* in the same syllable; as *phlegm, feign.*

3. *H* is silent after *G* or *R* at the beginning of a word; as *ghost, rhyme:* after *R* at the end of a word; as *myrrh;* and after a vowel at the end of a word; as *oh, Shi-loh, Sa-rah.*

4. *K* is always silent before *N* in the same syllable; as *knot, knob.*

5. *L* is silent in the terminations -*lk*, -*lm* following *a* or *o* in the same syllable; as *balk, balm, folk;* also in *could, would,* and *should,* pronounced *cood, wood,* and *shood.*

6. *N* is silent in the terminations *ln* and *mn;* as *kiln, hymn.*

7. *P* is silent when it precedes *s* or *t* in the same syllable; as *psalm, pti-san;* also between *m* and *t;* as *emp-ty, tempt.*

8. *T* is silent in the terminations *-tle* and *-ten* following *s*, the *e* being also dropped; as, *cas-tle, fas-ten,* pronounced *cas'l, fas'n.* *Th* is silent in *clothes.* EXCEPTION.—In *pes-tle* the *t* is sounded.

9. *W* is always silent before *r*, and before *h* followed by a long *o;* as *wry, whole.*

10. Both letters of the diphthong *ue* are silent at the end of words after *g* and *q*, except in *a-gue* and *ar-gue.*

No. 106—CVI.

B silent.

jamb	bomb	tomb	debt
lamb	(*bum*)	(*toom*)	doubt
limb	comb	numb	re doubt
climb	(*kome*)	crumb	sub tle
(*clime*)	dumb	plumb	debt or

C and Ch silent.

czar	drachm	yacht	vic tuals	in dict
cza ri na	schism	(*yot*)	(*vit tlz*)	(*dite*)
(*ree*)				

D silent.

Wed nes day	hand some	Darm stadt
(*wenz*)	Cron·stadt	stadt hold or

G silent.

CAUTION.—Do not say *de-zign*, but *de-sign;* nor *sauv-er-in,* but *suv-er-in.*

phlegm	im pregn*	im pugn	poign' ant
gnat	con dign	op pugn	seign' or
gnarl	be nign	pro pugn	se ragl' io
gnash	ma lign	ar raign	in tagl' io
gnaw	as sign	cam paign	di' a phragm
feign	de sign	bagn' io	par' a digm
reign	con sign	for' eign	ap' o (ph)thegm
sign	re sign	gno' men	sov' er eign
deign	ex pugn	gnos' tic	(*suv-er-in*)

---

* In this and the following eleven words, the silent *g* lengthens the preceding vowel.

H silent.

burgh	asth′ ma	naph′ tha	rhet′ o ric
ghost	burgh′ er	(nap)	rheu′ ma tism
heir	isth′ mus	rhu′ barb	(roo)
herb	diph′ thong*	Jeph′ thah	oph thal′ mic
hour	(dip)	Jo′ nah	(op)
myrrh	triph′ thong*	Mi′ cah	A bi′ jah
(mer)	(trip)	No′ ah	E li′ jah
rheum	ghast′ ly	Sa′ rah	J o si′ ah
(room)	gher′ kin	Thom′ as	Hez e ki′ ah
Rhine	heir′ ess	hon′ es ty	Jer e mi′ ah
Rhone	herb′ age	hos′ pi tal†	Ne he mi′ ah
rhomb	hon′ est	hu′ mor ous	Zech a ri′ ah
rhyme	hon′ or	oph′ thal my	Zeph a ni′ ah
thyme	hum′ ble†	(op)	hal le lu′ jah
sor′ ghum	hu′ mor	rhap′ so dy	(loo yah)

CAUTION.—Do not drop the *h* after *w*, when it should be strongly aspirated. To guard against this, pronounce the *h* before the *w*; thus, pronounce *what hoo-at, whet hoo-et.*

Practise reading and spelling the following words:

what wat	where wear	whin win	whine wine
when wen	whey way	whit wit	white wight
whet wet	whig wig	whist wist	why wye
wheel weal	which witch	while wile	wheth er weath er

K silent.

knack	kneel	knight	knoll	know
knave	knell	knit	(nole)	knap′ sack
knead	knew	knot	knob	knowl′ edge
knee	knife	knock	knout	knuc′ kle

* This is the pronunciation given by Walker and Worcester, and sanctioned by general usage. Webster gives *dif-thong* and *trif-thong.*

† *Hum-ble* and *hos-pi-tal* are sometimes heard with the *h* aspirated.

L silent.

NOTE.—A before *lk* is like *a* in *all*; before *lm* generally like *a* in *far*, sometimes like *a* in *fat*.

alms	halve	talk	could	palm y
balm	palm	walk	would	(p)salm ist
calf	(p)salm	*ch*alk	should	palm er
calve	qualm	stalk	calm cr	salm on
calm	balk	folk	calm est	
half	calk	(*foke*)	malm sey	

Instead of *yolk* (*yoke*), we generally find *yelk*.

M and N silent.

kiln	hymn	col umn	con demn	mne mon ics
limn	sol emn	au tumn	con temn	

P and Ph silent.

pshaw	psalm ist†	pti *s*an	per emp to ry*
psalm	psal ter	ex emp tion	phthi sis
prompt	(*saul*)	con sump tion	(*thi sis*)
tempt	at tempt	pre *s*ump tion	or
emp ty	con tempt	pneu mat ics	(*te zis*)
semp stress	ex empt	psalm o dy†	apo phthegm
symp tom	re ceipt	rasp ber rȳ	phthis ic
pseu do	(*seet*)	pre *s*ump tu ous	(*tiz ic*)

S silent.

aisle	sous	corps	isl and	de mesne
isle	(*sou*)	(*kore*)	vis count	a pro pos

---

* Avoid pronouncing this word with the accent on the second syllable instead of the first; still more, avoid pronouncing the first syllable *pre* instead of *per*.

† *Psalmist* and *psalmody* are pronounced either with or without the *L*; the latter generally with it.

T silent.

cas tle	thros tle	lis ten	cur rant
nes tle	bus tle	glis ten	mis tle toe
tres tle	jus tle	chris ten	gout
(w)res tle	rus tle	mois ten	(goo)
this tle	a pos tle*	of ten*	ra gout'
whis tle	e pis tle*	chest nut	(goo)
bris tle	fas ten	christ mas	haut' boy
gris tle	has ten	mort gage	(ho)
jos tle	chas ten	hos tler	

W silent.

wrap	wrench	wrought	whose	wres tle
wrack	wretch	wry	(hooz)	wrig gle
wrath	wright	sword	whole	wrin kle
wreak	wring	wroth	whole some	a wry'
wreath	wrist	who	tow ard	be wray'
wreck	write	(hoo)	tow ards	an swer
wren	writhe	whom	frow ard	
wrest	wrong	(hoom)	wran gle	

W is not silent in *whoop.*

CAUTION.—Do not drop the *w* in the second syllable of *awk-ward.* *Awk-erd* is a vulgarism.

UE silent.

Hague	ogue=og	ped a gogue	pic tu resque
vague	ec logue	syn a gogue	pique
plague	prol ogue	qu=k; i=ee	cri tique
league	ap o logue	cinque	u nique
fugue	cat a logue	mosque	fa tigue
rogue	di a logue	masque	in trigue
vogue	dec a logue	o paque	tongue
brogue	dem a gogue	o blique	(tung)
pro rogue'	ep i logue	bur lesque	ha rangue
col league'	mon o logue	gro tesque	

* We sometimes hear *apostle* and *epistle* with the *t*, perhaps to show their Greek origin. It has also become fashionable to sound the *t* in *often.* All these pronunciations are anomalous, and none of them is authorized or even noticed by any of our lexicographers.

GH silent.

-igh, -eigh = *i long.*	fright (w)right	in veigh *ough*=*oo*	taught fraught
high	blight	through	daugh ter
nigh	flight	through out	. haugh ty
sigh	plight	*ough*=*o*	us que baugh
bight	slight	dough	ought
dight	height	*though*	bought
fight	sleight	fur lough	fought
hight	*eigh*=*a*	bor ough	nought
light	*long.*	(*bur*)	sought
might	neigh	thor ough	brought
night	sleigh	(*thur*)	wrought
right	eight	al *though*	thought
sight	weight	*augh, ough*=*aw*	*ough*=*ou*
tight	freight	aught	bough
wight	eighth	caught	plough
bright	neigh bor	naught	slough

No. 107—CVII.

Point out the words which have silent letters.

No hon-est man will in-cur a debt, un-less he knows
    he will be a-ble to pay it.

Dough ought to be thor-ough-ly wrought, so as
    to make bread light.

Lis-ten to the mock-ing bird whis-tling on that
    bough.

It is wrong to fright-en chil-dren by tell-ing them
    sto-ries about ghosts.

Af-ter a great bat-tle has been fought, the hos-pi-tals
    with-in reach are filled with wound-ed sol-diers
    (*sole-jers*).

Sal-mon is a de-li-cious fish to eat; but it is not
    caught in our south ern wa-ters.

The pain of rheu-ma-tism is of-ten so se-vere as to
    de form the limbs.

John fell in-to a slough, and got out in a sad plight.

Fas-ten a hal-ser to the yacht, and haul her a-shore
    that we may have her calked to make her seams
    tight.

Myrrh is a gum im-ported from Tur-key. The best
rhu-barb is al-so called Tur-key rhu-barb; but all
our rhu-barb is cul-ti-va-ted in Chi-na.

The knout is an in-stru-ment of pun-ish-ment used
in Rus-sia. It is made of a strip of hide har-dened
by soak-ing it in milk and dry-ing it in the sun.

Sev-er-al sys-tems of mne-mon-ics have been in-
vent-ed, ap-plied chief-ly to chro-nol-o-gy; but
none of them has an-swered its pur-pose so well
as to be-brought in-to gen-er-al use. A good
mem-o-ry can do its work with-out them; and
a bad one is on-ly per-plex-ed by them.

A gen-er-al of-ten ha-rangues his sol-diers be-fore
lead-ing them in-to the fight.

The love of God and of our neigh-bor is the sum of
all the com-mand-ments con-tained in the Dec-a-
logue.

"A soft an-swer turn-eth away wrath."

Chalk is found in a-bun-dance in the chalk hills in
the south of En-gland (*Ing-gland*), and flint is al-
ways found with it.

Christ-mas is the birth-day of Christ. It comes in
the mid-dle of our win-ter; and is ob-served
ev-er-y where as a day of feast-ing and re-
joic-ing.

Be-hold, a rain-cloud hangs in the sky, and the sun
is look-ing up-on it from the oth-er side of heav-en;
and now, a lof-ty arch of man-y col-ors ap-pears to
our view. That cloud is made of rain drops; and
the beams of the sun, shi-ning on them and turned
back to the eye, seem like a bow paint-ed on the
cloud.

Look up-on the rain-bow, and praise Him who made
it. The hands of the Most High have bent it;
and there it hangs, a faith-ful wit-ness of the truth
of God.

"I do set my bow in the cloud, and it shall be for a
to-ken of a cov-e-nant be-tween me and the earth.
And it shall come to pass, when I bring a cloud
o-ver the earth, that the bow shall be seen in the
cloud."—[*Pictorial Tract Primer.*

PART II.
APPLICATION AND FURTHER DEVELOPMENT OF ELEMENTARY PRINCIPLES.

No. 108—CVIII.

The learner may now begin to analyze a few words in each lesson, stating the vowel sounds and the variable consonant sounds, with the reasons as far as he is acquainted with them. A table of these sounds is annexed.

VOWEL SOUNDS.

A has four sounds.

1 The long *a*, as in *fate*, with its shortened sound as in va-*cate*.

2. The Italian *a*, as in *far*, with its shortened sound as in *grasp*.

3. The broad *a*, as in *all*, with its shortened sound as in *was*.

4. The short *a*, as in *fat*.

E has two sounds.

1. The long *e*, as in *me*, with its shortened sound as in *re*-vere.

2. The short *e*, as in *met*.

I has two sounds.

1. The long diphthongal *i* (*ah-ee*), as in *pine*.

2. The short *i*, as in *pin*.

O has four sounds.

1. The long open *o*, as in *no*, with its shortened sound as in *pro*-mote.

2. The long close *o*, as in *move*.

3. The long broad *o*, as in *nor*.

4. The short broad *o*, as in *not*.

U has three sounds.

1. The long diphthongal *u* (*ee-oo*) as in *tube*, with its shortened sound as in fu-*ture*.

2. The short *u*, as in *tub*.

3. The middle or obtuse *u* as in *bull*, with its shortened sound as in *bush*.

The diphthong *oi* is compounded of the sounds *aw* and *ee*—the broad *a* and the long *e*, as in *oil*.

The diphthong *ou* is compounded of the sounds *aw* and *oo*—the broad *a* and the obtuse *u*, as in *thou*.

C is *soft* like *s*, as in *city*.
    hard like *k*, as in *card*.
G is *soft* like *j*, as in *gin*.
    hard as in *gun*.
S is *sharp* as in *this*.
    flat as in *is*.
Ch is *soft* like *tsh*, as in *church*.
    hard like *k*, as in *chord*.
Th is *sharp*, as in *thin*.
    flat, as in *this*.
X is *sharp* like *ks*, as in *exit*.
    flat like *gz*, as in *exist*.

No. 109—CIX.
RULES.

The following rules may be committed to memory, or they may be merely referred to. Frequent reference will soon render them familiar.

1. A vowel ending an accented syllable has its long or name sound; as, *pa-per*, *to-per*.

2. A vowel followed by a single consonant and a silent *e*, has its long or name sound; as, *tame*, *time*, *tune*.

3. *A* ending an unaccented syllable sounds like *a* in *fat*; as, *a-bout*, *a-round*; with a few exceptions; as, *Is-ra-el*. The article *A* should never be pronounced like *ay* unless it is accented or emphatic. Do not say "ay book," but "ah book."

4. *I* or *Y* ending an unaccented syllable, sounds like the long *e*; as, *lev-i-ty* (*lev-e te*); except in the termination *fy*; as, *grat-i-fy*.

5. *C* and *G* are generally soft, before *e, i* and *y,* and hard in other positions; as, cit-y, cart-er; gin, gun.

6. The prefix *ex* has *x* flat like *gz*, when followed by an accented syllable beginning with a vowel or *h ;* in other positions sharp like *ks ;* as, *ex-ist* (*egz-ist*), *ex-hort* (*egz-hort*), *ex-it* (*eks-it*).

The following is an example of the analysis of words which may now be required of the learner.

Ec-cen-tric. E, c—ec ; c, e, n—cen ; ec-cen ; t, r, i, c —tric ; ec-cen-tric ; accent on the second syllable *cen.* First syllable—*e* short sound as in *met, c* hard because not followed by *e, i,* or *y.* Second syllable—*c* soft because followed by *e, e* short sound as in *met.* Third syllable—*i* short sound as in *pin, c* hard because not followed by *e, i,* or *y.*

Those teachers who have not tried this exercise, will find it much easier, even to very young learners, than might at first be supposed. Its great utility and advantage are manifest.

No. 110—CX. *-tion, -sion, etc.*

-Cion, -tion, and *-sion,* are pronounced *shun* (not *shin*) ; and *-xion* is pronounced *k-shun.*

But *-tion* after *s* or *x* is pronounced *tyun ;* and *-sion* after a vowel is pronounced *zhun.*

Two Syllables. Accent on first.

na tion	dic tion	pen sion	hal cyon
sta tion	fic tion	ten sion	flex ion
lo tion ,	auc tion	spon sion	flux ion
mo tion	sanc tion	ver sion	ax iom
no tion •	unc tion	pas sion	fash ion
po tion	junc tion	ces sion	cush ion
cau tion	men tion	ses sion	vi sion
ac tion	cap tion	mis sion	(vizh un)
fac tion	op tion	scis sion	fu sion
frac tion	por tion	(siz zhun)	(zhun)
pac tion	man sion	fal chion	quos tion
sec tion	scan sion	(faul shun)	mix tion

No. 111—CXI.

Gi, Ge=J; Ci, Ti, Sci=Sh.

Two Syllables.   Accent on first.

le gion	lun cheon	con science	pa tient
re gion	pun cheon	mar tial	tran sient*
dun geon	styg ian	par tial	(*shent*)
dud geon	cap tious	nup tial	spe cies
gud geon	cau tious	cru cial	(*sheze*)
pi geon	gra cious	so cial	o cean
wid geon	spa cious	spe cial	(*o shan*)
bour geon	spe cious	(*spesh al*)	fus tian
(*bur*)	lus cious	an cient	(*tyan*)
sur geon	con scious	(*ain shent*)	bes tial
stur geon	anx ious	quo tient	(*tyal*)
scutch éon	nox ious	(*kwo shent*)	

No. 112—CXII.   -ition, -ision, ician, etc.

Three Syllables.   Accent on Second.

-ition=ish-un.		di vi sion	-tion after s and x
ad di tion	pe ti tion	e li sion	ad mix tion
am bi tion	po si tion	ex ci sion	ad us tion
at tri tion	se di tion	in ci sion	com bus tion
con di tion	sus pi cion	pro vi sion	com mix tion
con tri tion	tu i tion	re vi sion	con ges tion
den ti tion	ven di tion	xion=k-shun.	di ges tion
e di tion	vo li tion	com plex ion	ex haus tion†
ig ni tion	-ision=izh-un.	con nex ion	sug ges tion
in si tion	al li sion	ician=ish-an.	
mu ni tion	col li sion	lo gi cian	
nu tri tion	de ci sion	ma gi cian	re li gion
par ti tion	de ri sion	phy si cian	e ly sian

* Not *tran-zhent*.
† Remember that the *H* is aspirated. Pronounce *ege-haus-tyun*, not *ege-aus-tyun*. See CAUTION, No. 99.

No. 113—CXIII.   -tion, -sion.

Three Syllables; primitives two.   Accent on Second.

at tract	at trac tion	de sert	de ser tion
con tract	con trac tion	ex ert	ex er tion
de tract	de trac tion	pre sume	pre sump tion
ex. tract	ex trac tion	re sume	re sump tion
ex act	ex ac tion	de duce	de duc tion
trans act	trans ac tion	re duce	re duc tion
re fract	re frac tion	pro duce	pro duc tion
sub tract	sub trac tion	con vene	con ven tion
col lect	col lec tion	de ceive	de cep tion
cor rect	cor rec tion	per ceive	per cep tion
de tect	de tec tion	re ceive	re cep tion
di rect	di rec tion	de tain	de ten tion
dis sect	dis sec tion	re tain	re ten tion
e lect	e lec tion	de stroy	de struc tion
in fect	in fec tion	con fess	con fes sion
in spect	in spec tion	di gress	di gres sion
ex cept	ex cep tion	pro gress	pro gres sion
ex empt	ex emp tion	dis cuss	dis cus sion
af flict	af flic tion	pos sess	pos ses sion
con vict	con vic tion	op press	op pres sion
pre dict	pre dic tion	trans gress	trans gres sion
re strict	re stric tion	ad mit	ad mis sion
dis tinct	dis tinc tion	re mit	re mis sion
in vent	in ven tion	a scend	a scen sion
pre vent	pre ven tion	de scend	de scen sion
con struct	con struc tion	ex tend	ex ten sion
in struct	in struc tion	pre tend	pre ten sion
ob struct	ob struc tion	sus pend	sus pen sion
ad opt	ad op tion	a vert	a ver sion
con tort	con tor tion	per vert	per ver sion
dis tort	dis tor tion	dis perse	dis per sion
ex tort	ex tor tion	im merse	im mer sion
ab sorb	ab sorp tion	com mit	com mis sion
con tend	con ten tion	de cline	de clen sion
in tend	in ten tion	se cede	se ces sion
cre ate	cre a tion	pro ceed	pro ces sion
re late	re la tion	sub merge	sub mer sion
trans late	trans la tion	pro pel	pro pul sion
com plete	com ple tion	re pel	re pul sion

rc plate	re ple tion	*sion* after a vowel=*zhun.*	
se crete	se cre tion	ad here	ad he sion
de vote	de vo tion	co here	co he sion
pro mote	pro mo tion	al lude	al lu sion
pol lute	pol lu tion	de lude	de lu sion
a scribe	a scrip tion	per suade	per sua sion
con scribe	con scrip tion	ex plode	ex plo sion
sub scribe	sub scrip tion	pro trude	pro tru sion
as sume	as sump tion	re scind	re scis sion
con sume	con sump tion	ab scind	ab scis sion
as sert	as ser tion	co erce	co er cion

No. 114—CXIV.

Ac-cent is the stress of voice placed on one syl-la ble of
a word a-bove the oth-er syl la-bles; and the syl-la ble
so marked is called the ac-cent-ed syl la ble.

In the words in *-tion* and *-sion* giv-en in the two pre-ce
ding num bers, the ac cent is on the sec-ond syl-la-ble
as it is in all words of three syl-la bles with these endings. In some such words the ac-cent of the primi
tive is changed, but not in man y; as, *lo'-cate, lo-ca'-tion;
per'-fect, per-fec'-tion.*

Some-times rail-road cars run-ning rap-id-ly in op po-site
di-rec-tions come in-to col li-sion with each oth-er.
Of-ten, on such oc-ca-sions, man y lives are lost, and
of the sur-vi-vors man-y are dis a-bled. How great
care should be ta-ken to pre-vent such dis-tress-ing
ac-ci-dents!

A-void de-cep-tion. De-cep-tion is in-tend ed to make
oth-ers be-lieve some-thing which is not the truth.
All de-cep-tion, there-fore, wheth-er in word or deed,
is, in plain terms, ly-ing. Read what the Bible says:
"What man is he that de-si-reth life, and lov-eth man-y
days, that he may see good? Keep thy tongue (*tung*)
from e-vil, and thy lips from speak ing guile. De-part
from e-vil, and do good: seek peace, and pur-sue it."

Steam, if ad-mit-ted in-to a ves-sel whence it can-not
have free out-let, will *force* its way out, and thus pro-
duce an ex-plo-sion, as in the boil-ers of steam-en-
gines in which steam is, from any cause, gen-er-a-
ted too rap-id-ly.

To pre-dict is to fore-tell; that is, to tell the com-ing of an e-vent which is yet fu ture. No man could pre-dict tru-ly un-less God re-vealed the com-ing e-vent to him, or, in oth-er words, un-less he were in-spired, as were the old proph-ets whose pre-dic-tions you will read in the Ho-ly Scrip-tures when you shall have learned to read well. If you can-not read ea-si-ly and cor-rect-ly, you are de-prived of read-ing good books, and you can learn noth-ing else, for read-ing is the key to all learn-ing.

The Earth on which we live is one of the plan-ets of what we call the So-lar System. It moves round the Sun in a track or path called its or-bit, and so marks the year; while at the same time it moves round its own ax-is, as a top moves round when you spin it, and by this mo-tion it marks the day.

Cre-a-tion is ma king some-thing out of noth ing. It is call-ing in-to be-ing that which did not ex-ist in an-y shape be-fore. Man can change the forms of the ob-jects which are a-round him; he can make the square round, and the round square; he can com-bine the sub-stan-ces which are in his pow-er, so as to pro-duce oth-er sub stan-ces new to him: but to bring in-to be-ing one at-om of mat-ter which be-fore had no be-ing, be-longs on-ly to God. He alone "spake and it was done; he com-mand-ed and it stood fast."

A pen-sion is a sal-a-ry or year-ly pay ment for past ser-vi-ces.

An auc-tion is a pub-lic sale of goods to the high-est bid-der. You hear the auc-tion-eer cry "go-ing, go-ing;" but when he says "gone," no more bids will be re-ceived for that ar-ti-cle.

The con—struc-tion, that is, the put—ting to—geth—er, of a sen-tence, must not be de-stroyed by the read—ing of it. First: be well as—sured that you know all the words in the sen-tence be—fore you pre—tend to read it, that you may not be o—bliged to stop to find out what the next word is; then, read to-geth-er, with—out paus-ing be—tween them, those words which are con—nect-ed with each oth—er in the sense.

No. 115.—CXV. -et, -it, -ot, -en, -in, -on, etc.

Two Syllables. Accent on first.

com bat	cut let	asp en	gal lon
ban quet	pack et	bar ren	gam mon
car pet	pel let	chick en	gor gon
cir clet	plum met	hy men	pa tron
cors let	pock et	hy phen	sci on
cros set	proph et	kitch en	sex ton
crotch et	pul let	lent en	squad ron
doub let	pup pet	lin den	ster non
drug get	rock et	lin en	sy phon
dul cet	rus set	sy ren	ten don
ea glet	sig net	war ren	bit tern
fau cet	skil let	bod kin	cis tern
fer ret	tab let	bus kin	east ern
fil let	tar get	dau phin	lan tern
front let	thick et	dol phin	pat tern
gaunt let	tick et	fir kin	pos tern
gib bet	tip pet	gob lin	quar tern
gim let	trip let	grif fin	slat tern
gus set	tur ret	jer kin	stub born
hatch et	vel vet	mar gin	blan dish
hor net	wick et	muf fin	bran dish
in let	com fit	mus lin	bur nish
jack et	com fort	nap kin	churl ish
jen net	her mit	pip pin	girl ish
lan cet	plau dit	ur chin	fur bish
lap pet	rab bit	vir gin	fur nish
lin net	trans it	bea con	gar nish
lock et	u nit	cal dron	pub lish
mal let	car rot	can non	elf ish
mar ket	in got	can ton	self ish
mil let	par rot	ca pon	skir mish
mul let	cr got	com mon	skit tish
off set	guar dian*	de mon	tar nish
on set	or gan	mam mon	var nish
out set	tar tan	mor mon	book ish
rab bet	o men	ser mon	boor ish

* Pronounced also in three syllables—*gar-de-an*; but not
gar-deen.'

No. 116—CXVI.

The following have the vowel in the accented syllable short, though followed by a single consonant only.

car at	prof it	sat in	cav ern
duc at	tac it	bar on	tav ern
civ et	vis it	can on	ban ish
clar et	big ot	drag on	blem ish
clos et	spig ot	eb on	cher ish
com et	pat en	fel on	fam ish
cov et	plat en	flag on	fin ish
plan et	cab in	her on	lav ish
priv et	cum in	lem on	par ish
spin et	lat in	mel on	pol ish
deb it	mat in	tal on	pun ish
des ert	rav in	ten on	rad ish
dig it	rob in	wag on	rel ish
mer it	ros in	weap on	van ish

NOTE.—*A-men* and *fare-well* are accented on both syllables.

No. 117—CXVII.   -en, -on='n.

ba con	deep en	lead en	par don	sick en
bat ten	doz en	leav en	poi son	slov en
beat en	earth en	less en	per son	(sluv'n)
bid den	e ven	les son	pris on	smit ten
bla zon	fat ten	light en	quick en	sod den
bra zen	flat ten	li ken	rai sin	sweet en
bro ken	gar den	loos en	ra ven	ta ken
but ton	glad den	mad den	rav en	thick en
cheap en	glut ton	maid en	rea son	threat en
clo ven	gold en	ma son	reck on	treas on
cot ton	hap pen	miz zen	sev en	vix en
cous in	ha ven	molt en	sad den	wax en
coz en	hea then	mut ton	seas on	weak en
dark en	heav en	oak en	sharp en	writ ten
dead en	kit ten	ov en(uv'n)	ox en	hard en

No. 118—CXVIII.

Silent E preceded by a single consonant and a single vowel.

Two Syllables. Accent on first.

*Shortened sound of the long a: -ace, -age, -ate, etc.**

fur nace	im age	ton nage	prel ate
men ace	lan guage	um brage	pro bate
pal ace	leak age	vin tage	quad rate
pref ace	man age	vis age	sen ate
pur chase	mar r(i)age	voy age	stag nate
ter race	mes sage	ag ate	va cate
ad age	mes suage	ce rate	vul gate
bag gage	out rage	cu rate	com rade
ban dage	pas sage	fil trate.	(kum rade)
bon dage	peer age	frig ate	dec ade
car nage	pil lage	frus trate	bel dame
car r(i)age	plu mage	in nate	mem brane
cot tage	pound age	leg ate	war fare
dam age	pres age	man date	wel fare
for age	sav age	mess mate	con cave
fruit age	stow age	nar rate	con clave
hom age	suf frage.	or nate	col lege
hos tage	til lage	pal ate	ves tige
coin age	cord age	cog nate	oc tave
cour age	pack age	mi grate	pul sate
non age	sal vage	pi rate	pri vate
rav age	sau sage	pro late	sol ace
sel vage	van tage	ship mate	spin age

* In many of these words, this sound is given in our dictionaries as that of the short *i;* probably because, when we give the *a* its proper sound, as in the second syllable of *vacate*, it approaches the short *i* in the rapidity of pronunciation.

5

-ice, -ise, -ile, -ine, -ive, etc.

ice, ise=iss	prom ise	doc trine	ex ile
aus pice .	*ile=ill*	en gine*	gen tile
bod ice	ag ile	jas mine	se nile
chal ice	doc ile	pris tine	vir ile
cop pice	duc tile	rap ine	pas time
cor nice	fac ile	san guine	quin ine†
crev ice	feb rile	vac cine	bon fire
jus tice	fer tile	*ive=iv*	em pire
lat tice	flex ile	fes tive	um pire
mal ice	fu tile	fur tive	sat ire†
nov ice	grac ile	mas sive	con trite
poul tice	mis sile	mis sive	fi nite
(*pole*)	nu bile	mo tive	le vite
prac tice	rep tile	na tive	
pum ice	ser vile	pas sive	gran ite
ser vice	sex tile	plain tive	sam phire
sol stice	sub tile	sport ive .	(*fer*)
an ise	*ine=inn*	vo tive	sap phire
mor tise	alp ine	*i long*	(*saf fer*)
prac tise	des tine	e dile	con crete

Consonant before E doubled. | *Accent on second syllable.*

ga zelle	par terre	co quette	ve dette
ion quille	(*par tare*)	(*co ket*)	vig nette
(*jun kwil*)	du resse‡	cor vette	(*vih yet*)
qua drille	fi nesse	ga zette	
(*ka dril*)	bru nette	lu nette	.

---

* Not *in-jine* but *en-jin*.
† The ordinary pronunciation is given. See Worcester's Dictionary.
‡ Spelled also without the e.

U *long.*

a zure	nur ture	treas ure	ref use
fea ture	pas ture	ven ture	stat ute
fig ure	per jure	ver dure	trib ute
fix ture	pleas ure	ves ture	
frac ture	rap ture	prod uce	let tuce
fu ture	scis sure	prel ude	(*tis*)
in jure	(*siz zhoor*)	del uge	min ute
junc ture	scrip ture	ref uge	(*it*)
lec ture	sei zure	per uke	ful some
lei sure	stat ure	glob ule	in come
(*lee zhoor*)	struc ture	pus tule	irk some
meas ure	tex ture	sched ule	loa*th* some
mix ture	tinc ture	cos tume	noi some
mois ture	ton sure	per fume	tire some
na ture	tor ture	for tune	there fore*

No. 119—CXIX.

A lit-tle boy had two pet rab-bits, and it af ford-ed him
great pleas-ure to feed them sev-er-al times a day, and
to have them come to him when he called, "bun-ny,
bun-ny." But they e-scaped some how, or per haps
were sto len. At all e vents, he could nev-er find
them a-gain.

What a han(d)-some car-pet that is! How much it will
im-prove the ap pear-ance of the par-lor, when it is
tacked down on the floor.

In old times, be fore the in-ven-tion of gun-pow-der, at
least be-fore it came in-to gen-er al use as a means of
de stroy-ing life, men of war wore cors lets, or close-
fit-ting coats made of steel or brass, to de-fend them-
selves a-gainst the at-tacks of their en-e-mies.

See the live ly lit-tle kit-ten, how it frol-ics. It will run
af-ter a ball, or play with a piece of thread; and now
it is try-ing to catch its own tail.

* Not *thair-fore*, but *ther-fore*, *e* as in *men.*

A tav-ern is a place where they sell whis-key, and rum, and beer, and oth-er drinks to make men drunk. I hope, my dear boy, you will never be a vis-it-er of tav-erns.

Did you ev-er see a pup-pet? It is a lit-tle doll or im-age of a man or wo-man, moved by wires. Sev-er-al of these pup-pets are shown for mon-ey, by a per-son who moves them and speaks for them, and so makes a great deal of fun. They per-form a mock play. Per haps you may some time have a chance of see-ing "Punch and Ju-dy."

A jen-net is a lit-tle Span ish po ny. Would you not like to have one to ride on with a nice sad-dle and bri-dle?

A crotch et is a mu-si-cal note. Some-times it means a whim or odd no-tion.

The in-side of a watch-glass is con-cave; the out side is con-vex.

You can not read well, or do an y thing well, with-out a great deal of prac-tice. It is an old ad-age that "prac-tice makes per-fect." Prac-tise, there fore, what-ev-er you wish to do per fect-ly.

There is fre-quent ly much more hap-pi-ness in a cot tage than in a pal-ace.

In Sep-tem-ber you may see the ne groes pick-ing cot-ton. Hark! how mer-ri-ly they sing as they pick the white cot-ton from the pods, and throw it in-to the bas-ket. These ne-groes are well fed, and well clad, and well cared for when they are sick. When their task is done, there is noth-ing to trou-ble them. Which of us that lives to an-y pur-pose, has not his task to do, as well as the ne-gro?

Can you tell the dif-fer-ence be-tween a voy-age and a jour-ney? If you can not, find it out, and you will nev-er for-get it.

Gran-ite is a hard rock used for build-ing. The fronts of man-y stores have gran-ite pil-lars. See the small specks in it that glit-ter so. - Those lit-tle specks are mi-ca.

Com-ets are not the same as plan-ets. Per-haps you may have seen a com-et. They are seen but rare-ly, and yet they are ver-y nu-mer-ous.

No. 120.—CXX. -tion, -sion.
Four Syllables. Accent on third.
Primitives three Syllables. Accent on first.

ag i tate	ag i ta tion	mod er ate	mod er a tion
con gre gate	con gre ga tion	mod u late	mod u la tion
con ju gate	con ju ga tion	nom i nate	nom i na tion
cul ti vate	cul ti va tion	op er ate	op er a tion
ded i cate	ded i ca tion	os cil late	os cil la tion
des o late	des o la tion	per fo rate	per fo ra tion
de vi ate	de vi a tion	prop a gate	prop a ga tion
ed u cate	ed u ca tion	reg u late	reg u la tion
ex tri cate *	ex tri ca tion	ren o vate	ren o va tion
fas ci nate	fas ci na tion	sep a rate	sep a ra tion
fu mi gate	fu mi ga tion	spec u late	spec u la tion
grad u ate	grad u a tion	ter mi nate	ter mi na tion
grav i tate	grav i ta tion	tol er ate	tol er a tion
im i tate	im i ta tion	un du late	un du la tion
im mo late	im mo la tion	vac ci nate	vac ci na tion
in ti mate	in ti ma tion	veg e tate	veg e ta tion
leg is late	leg is la tion	ven ti late	ven-ti la tion
lit i gate	lit i ga tion	con sti tute	con sti tu tion
me di ate	me di a tion	ex e cute	ex e cu tion
med i tate	med i ta tion	sub sti tute	sub sti tu tion

Primitives three Syllables. Accent on second.

com pen sate	com pen sa tion	dis trib ute	dis tri bu tion
con fis cate	con fis ca tion	di min ish	dim i nu tion
con tem plate	con tem pla tion	e lon gate*	el on ga tion
de mon strate*	de mon stra tion	ex tir pate	ex tir pa tion
ex tir pate	ex tir pa tion	il lus trate	il lus tra tion
con trib ute	con tri bu tion	se ques trate*	se ques tra tion

Primitives three Syllables. Accent on third.

ap pre hend	ap pre hen sion	man u mit	man u mis sion
com pre hend	com pre hen sion	mis con ceive	mis con cep tion
con de scend	con de scen sion	pre pos sess	pre pos ses sion
in ter mit	in ter mis sion	rec ol lect	rec ol lec tion
in ter vene	in ter ven tion	rep re hend	rep re hen sion
in tro duce	in tro duc tion	in ter sect	in ter sec tion

* The learner should be led to notice that in the words marked with an asterisk, the long vowel in the first syllable of the primitive becomes short in the first syllable of the derivative.

~It may also be observed, as a *cautionary remark*, that the first five and the last but one of the primitives of three syllables, accented on the second, are liable to mispronunciation by removing the accent to the first; as, *com'-pen-sate*, for *com-pen'-sate*, etc.

Primitives two Syllables. Accent on second.

ac cept	ac cep ta tion	o blige	ob li ga tion
ac claim	ac cla ma tion	or dain	or di na tion
ac cuse	ac cu sa tion	pro claim*	proc la ma tion
ad apt	ad ap ta tion	pro long*	prol on ga tion
al lege	al le ga tion	re pair*	rep a ra tion
ap ply	ap pli ca tion	trans form	trans for ma tion
com bine	com bi na tion	trans port	trans por ta tion
com mute	com mu ta tion	u surp	u sur pa tion
con geal	con ge la tion	ad ore	ad o ra tion
de claim*	dec la ma tion	af firm	af fir ma tion
de rive*	der i va tion	ex pect	ex pec ta tion
dis pense	dis pen sa tion	pro voke*	prov o ca tion
fer ment	fer men ta tion	dis solve	dis so lu tion
in cline	in cli na tion	e volve*	ev o lu tion
in spire	in spi ra tion	in volve	in vo lu tion
mo lest*	mol es ta tion	re solve*	res o lu tion

Five Syllables. Accent on fourth.

Primitives four Syllables. Accent on second.

ab bre vi ate	–a tion	e nun ci ate	–a tion
ac cel er ate	–a tion	e vap or rate	–ra tion
ac cen tu ate	–a tion	ex ag ger ate	–a tion
ac cu mu late	–la tion	fa cil i tate	–ta tion
al le vi ate	–a tion	fe lic i tate	–ta tion
an ni hi late	–la tion	ges tic u late	–la tion
an tic i pate	–pa tion	in cor po rate	–ra tion
ap pre ciate	–a tion	in sin u ate	–a tion
ap prox i mate	–ma tion	in ter ro gate	–ga tion
as sim i late	–la tion	in tox i cate	–ca tion
ca pit u late	–la tion	in vig o rate	–ra tion
com mem o rate	–ra tion	ne go ti ate	–a tion
con cil i ate	–a tion	ob lit er ate	–a tion
con sol i date	–da tion	o rig i nate	–na tion
co op er ate	–a tion	par tic i pate	–pa tion
cor rob o rate	–ra tion	pro cras ti nate	–na tion
de lib er ate	–a tion	pro pi ti ate	–a tion
de pop u late	–la tion	re it er ate	–a tion
de pre ci ate	–a tion	sub or di nate	–na tion
e ma ci ate	–a tion	vi tu per ate	–a tion

Six Syllables. Accent on fifth.

al co hol i za tion	per son i fi ca tion
be a tif i ca tion	ra ti oc i na tion
cir cum nav i ga tion	re ca pit u la tion
con sub stan ti a tion	rec on cil i a tion
de te ri o ra tion	su per er o ga tion
ex com mu ni ca tion	tran sub stan ti a tion
in dem ni fi ca tion	*Seven Syllables.*
in ter lin e a tion	spir it u al i za tion

-ition=ish-un.

ab o li tion	dep o si tion	im po si tion
ac qui si tion	dis po si tion	in qui si tion
ad mo ni tion	eb ul li tion	op po si tion
am mu ni tion	er u di tion	prep o si tion
ap pa ri tion	ex hi bi tion	prop o si tion
op po si tion	pro hi bi tion	rec og ni tion
co a li tion	ex pe di tion	rep e ti tion
com po si tion	ex po si tion	re qui si tion
def i ni tion	sup po si tion	*(rek we)*
dem o li tion	trans po si tion	cir cum ci sion

No. 121.—CXXI.

We have now ar-rived at words of four, five, and six syl-la-bles. The spell-ing les-sons must be read care-ful-ly and fre-quent-ly, as read-ing les-sons. Read four words, and then four more, and so on, end-ing each time as if you were read-ing a sen-tence. See that you leave out no let-ter and no syl-la-ble that should be pro-nounced. Read slow-ly, and do not let the syl-la-bles run in-to each oth-er; but ob-serve the ver-y sim-ple rule, "*Fin-ish* each syl-la-ble and each word, be-fore you be-gin an-oth-er syl-la-ble or an-oth-er word," and you will soon read dis-tinct-ly.

Re-ceive the ad mo ni tions of your teach ers with re-spect and sub mis sion. They are, for the time, in the place of your pa rents; and you should be have to-wards them as to wards those who are anx-ious to do you ser vice.

The two words *fa cil i-tate* and *fe lic i-tate* are ver y like each oth-er: but words which re sem ble each oth er ver-y much in sound, fre quent ly dif fer great ly in mean ing. *Fa cil i-tate* means "*to make eas y;*" as, "Fre-quent rep e-ti tion will fa-cil i-tate your pro-gress." *Fe lic-i-tate* means "to ex press pleas ure to a friend on ac-count of some for-tu nate thing that has hap pened to him."

To put off or de fer what you should do now, till to-mor-row; and then a gain till the next day, and so on, is to pro-cras ti nate. "What-so ev-er thy hand find-eth to do, do it with thy might." One of our po ets says—

"Pro-cras-ti-na-tion is the thief of time:
Year af-ter year it steals, till all are fled."

When a wit-ness comes for-ward on a tri al in a court of jus tice, the law yers in-ter ro gate him, some-times ver y strict ly, that is, they ask him a great man-y ques tions.

A phy si cian is not the same as a sur-geon. If a man is wound-ed, or if, by some ac ci-dent, his leg or his arm is bro ken, a sur-geon is sent for to treat the wound or the frac-ture. But if one has an-y dis-ease, as fe-ver and a gue or bil ious fe-ver, his treat ment must be placed in the hands of a phy-si-cian.

Punc-tu-a-tion is the prop er pla-cing of the points or stops used in read-ing, as the com-ma (,), the pe-ri-od (.), and-so-forth, which you will find in the be-gin-ning of this book. It re quires an in-ti mate ac-quaint-ance with gram-mar to en a-ble one to punc-tu-ate cor-rect ly.

The pe-ri-od marks the end of a sen-tence, and is the long-est stop, while the com-ma is the short-est. At the *com ma* you pause till you can count *one;* at the *semi-co-lon* (;) till you can count *two;* at the co lon (:) a lit-tle long-er than at the sem-i-co lon; and at the pe-ri-od, the in-ter-ro-ga-tion point (?) or the ex-cla-ma-tion p int (!) till you can count *four.*

No. 122—CXXII.

Final y=e; -ies=eze; -ied=ede—Shortened sound of the long E.

Two Syllables. Accent on first.

car ry	car ries	car ried	mar rý	mar ries	mar ried
cop y	cop ies	cop ied	pit y	pit ies	pit ied
dal ly	dal lies	dal lied	ral ly	ral lies	ral lied
en vy	en vies	en vied	sal ly	sal lies	sal lied
fan cy	fan cies	fan cied	stud y	stud ies	stud ied
glo ry	glo ries	glo ried	tal ly	tal lies	tal lied
hur ry	hur ries	hur ried	tar ry	tar ries	tar ried
lev y	lev ies	lev ied	wor ry	wor ries	wor ried

Three Syllables. Accent on first.

ec sta sy	ec sta sies	glos sary	glos sa ries
em bas sy	em bas sies	gran a ry*	gran a ries
her e sy.	her e sies	li bra ry	li bra ries
leg a cy	leg a cies	sal a ry	sal a ries
com e dy	com e dies	vo ta ry	vo ta ries
rhap so dy	rhap so dies	his to ry	his to ries
trag e dy	trag e dies	the o ry	the o ries
el e gy	el e gies	vic to ry	vic to ries
ef fi gy	ef fi gies	bis tour y	bis tour ies
prod i gy	prod i gies	ar te ry	ar te ries
fam i ly	fam i lies	bat ter y	bat ter ies
en e my	en e mies	for ger y	for ger ies
com pa ny	com pa nies	gal ler y	gal ler ies
lit a ny	lit a nies	mys ter y	mys ter ies
tyr an ny	tyr an nies	cen tu ry	cen tu ries
prog e ny	prog e nies	in ju ry	in ju ries
ag o ny	ag o nies	lux u ry	lux u ries
bal co ny	bal co nies	gai e ty	gai e ties†
eu pho ny	eu pho nies	quan ti ty	quan ti ties
cal um ny	cal um nies	pen al ty	pen al ties
can o py	can o pies	am nes ty	am nes ties
con tra ry	con tra ries	gal ax y	gal ax ies

* Not *grain'-a-ry.*

† Spelled also with y.

NOTE —*In-qui'-ry* is not found here. It is improperly accented on the first syllable.

Four Syllables. Accent on first.

.acy = as-sy.

con tu ma cy	in tri ca cy	ob du ra cy
ef fi ca cy	mag is tra cy	ob sti nacy

-ary = ar-ry.

CAUTION.—Do not pronounce *a-ry*, *ai-ry* or *er-ry*. Do not say. *ad-ver-sai-ry* or *ad-ver-ser-ry*, but *ad-ver-sar-ry*.

ad ver sa ry	em is sa ry	pul mo na ry
an ti qua ry	es tu a ry	sal u ta ry
ai bi tra ry	ex em pla ry	sanc tu a ry
a vi a ry	Feb ru a ry*	san gui na ry
cap il la ry	Jan u a ry*	sec re ta ry
com men ta ry	lap i da ry	sed en ta ry
com mis sa ry	lit er a ry	sta tion a ry
cor ol la ry	mer ce na ry	sub lu na ry
cus tom a ry	mil i ta ry	sump tu a ry
dic tion a ry	nec es sa ry	tem po ra ry
drom e da ry	or di na ry*	vol un ta ry
(*drum*)	plan et a ry	

-ery, ory = ur-ry.

cem e ter y	dil a tor y	pred a tor y
dys en ter y	dor mi tor y	pref a tor y
mil li ñer y	in ven tor y	prom is sor y
pres by ter y	mi gra tor y	prom on tor y
sta tion er y	mon i tor y	rep er tor y
al le gor y	nu ga tor y	ter ri tor y
am a tor y	per emp tor y*	trans i tor y
ap o plex y	ig no min y	or tho dox y
con tro ver sy	mel an chol y	or tho e py
hi er arch y	nec ro man cy	pyr o tech ny

* Avoid the pronunciations *ex-em'-pler-y*, *Feb'-u-er-ry*, *Jen'-ny-war-y*, *or'-na-ry*, and *per-emp'-to-ry*.

No. 123—CXXIII.

What a lux-u-ry it is to have ac-cess' to a large and well se-lect-ed li-bra-ry!

A glos-sa-ry is nec-es-sa-ry, to ex-plain man-y words which we meet with in au-thors of three or four cen-tu-ries past.

Or'-tho-e-py is the cor-rect pro-nun-ci-a-tion of words.

Cal-um-ny is false-hood of the most wick-ed kind. It aims at the ru-in of a man's rep-u-ta-tion by cru-el mis-rep-re-sen-ta-tions.

A drom-e-da-ry is a spe-cies of cam-el.

Jan-u-a-ry is the first month of the year. Can you tell the names of the twelve months? Here they are—

Jan'-u-a ry,	May,	Sep-tem-ber,
Feb'-ru-a ry,	June,	Oc-to'-ber.
March,	Ju-ly',	No-vem'-ber,
A'-pril;	Au'-gust,	De-cem'-ber.

The plan-et a ry sys-tem, or, as it is called, the So-lar sys tem, con-sists of a num-ber of bod-ies like this Earth of ours, which re-volve round the sun in pe-ri-ods of time dif-fer-ing ac-cord-ing to their dis tances.

Lit-er a-ry men most com-mon-ly lead a sed-en-ta ry life.

What a rep-er-tor-y is the En-glish lan-guage! What rich treas-ures it con tains of wis-dom and knowl-edge ! Let us en-deav-or to make some por-tion at least of the seim-meas u-ra-ble rich-es our own.

Ob-serve the dif-fer-ence be-tween *mon-i tor-y* and *mon-e-ta-ry*, *sta-tion-er-y* and *sta-tion-a-ry*, *mil-li-ner-y* and *mil-le-na-ry;* and try to make the dif-fer-ence per-cep-ti-ble in your pro-nun-ci-a-tion of the words.

It is mel-an-chol-y to see a youth, and a bove all, a youth en-dowed with high men-tal ca-pac-i-ties, wast ing in i-dle-ness and dis-si-pa-tion the sea son of his life du-ring which the seeds should be plant ed of fu-ture use-ful-ness and dis-tinc-tion.

Do not con-tract a hab-it of be-ing dil-a-tor y in your move-ments.

Pul-mo na-ry dis-eas-es are those which at-tack the lungs.

One of the most use-ful and im-por tant stud-ies is His-to ry. A bare out-line of its ru-di-ments is all that can be ob-tained at school. It re-quires years of pa-tient ap-pli-ca-tion to make a pro-found his-to-ri-an.

No. 124.—CXXIV

Final y=e; ity, -ety.
Four Syllables. Accent on Second.

CAUTION.—Be careful not to drop the *i* or the *e* before *ty*.

au dac i ty	vi tal i ty	au thor i ty
ca pac i ty	a gil i ty	pri or i ty
lo quac i ty	fra gil i ty	eu pid i ty
men dac i ty	do cil i ty	va lid i ty
ra pac i ty	duc til i ty	so lid i ty
sa gac i ty	fa cil i ty	ti mid i ty
ve rac i ty	fer til i ty	ra pid i ty
vi vac i ty	fi del i ty	stu pid i ty
vo rac i ty	gen til i ty	com mod i ty
du plic i ty	hos til i ty	ca lam i ty
fe lic i ty	hu mil i ty	ex trem i ty
pub lic i ty	mo bil i ty	prox im i ty
rus tic i ty	no bil i ty	sub lim i ty
sim plic i ty	ser vil i ty	anx i e ty
a troc i ty	sta bil i ty	so bri e ty
ve loc i ty	ste ril i ty	e bri e ty
a tal i ty	tran quil li ty	im pi e ty
for mal i ty	as per i ty	pro pri e ty
fru gal i ty	aus ter i ty	sa ti e ty
le gal i ty	dex ter i ty	so bri e ty
lo cal i ty	se ver i ty	so ci e ty
mo ral i ty	sin cer i ty	va ri e ty
mor tal i ty	pos ter i ty	an ti qui ty
neu tral i ty	pros per i ty	in i qui ty
plu ral i ty	ma jor i ty	ob li qui ty
re al i ty	mi nor i ty	u bi qui ty

a scend en cy	my thol o gy	phy lac ter y
con sist en cy	phi lol o gy	mis an thro py
de lin quen cy	phre nol o gy	phi lan thro py
de spon den cy	tau tol o gy	so lil o quy
e mer gen cy	the ol o gy	bi og ra phy
in elem en cy	mo nop o ly	chi rog ra phy
in sol ven cy	pó lyg a my	cos mog ra phy
con spir a cy	a cad e my	ge og ra phy
de moe ra cy	a nat o my	li thog ra phy
su prem a cy	as tron o my	or thog ra phy
a pos ta sy	e con o my	pho nog ra phy
hy poe ri sy	phle bot o my	pho tog ra phy
a nal o gy	ma hog a ny	ste nog ra phy
au thol o gy	cos mog o ny	to pog ra phy
chro nol o gy	mo not o ny	ty pog ra phy
dox ol o gy	ar til ler y	an tip a thy
ge ol o gy	chi ca ner y	a pos tro phe

No. 125—CXXV

Bi-og-ra-phy is the his-to-ry of the life of a par-tic-u-lar per-son.

Ge-og-ra-phy is to most chil-dren a ver-y pleas-ant stud-y.

Un-less peo-ple of mod-er-ate means prac-tise e-con-o-my, they may be re-duced to pov-er-ty.

Ma-hog-a-ny is a val-u-a-ble spe-cies of wood. Near-ly all our best fur-ni-ture is made of ma-hog-a-ny.

We must not un-der-take too great a va-ri-e-ty of stud-ies at once. If you put too man-y i-rons in the fire, ac-cord ing to an old say-ing, some of them must cool.

Ste-nog-ra-phy is a short meth-od of wri-ting. It is em-ployed in ta-king notes of speech-es at pub-lic meet-ings.

Nev-er go to school too late with-out an a-pol-o-gy.

Try to make to your-self a char-ac-ter for ve-rac-i-ty by nev-er de-part-ing from the truth.

The sa-gac-i-ty of man-y of the in fe-ri-or an-i-mals is sur-pri-sing. Tales are told, of the dog, the horse, and the el-e-phant; which make it hard to de-ny that they have the use of rea son.

Phi-lan-thro py and mis-an-thro-py are the op-po-
sites of each oth-er. Phi-lan-thro-py is the love
of man-kind. Mis-an-thro-py is the ha-tred of
man-kind.

No be-ing but God is pos sess-ed of u-bi-qui-ty.

Ra-pid-i-ty of cal-cu-la-tion is a val-u-a-ble ac-quire-
ment.

Rus-tic-i ty of man-ners with good-ness of heart, is
great-ly to be pre-ferred to that pol-ished el-e-
gance which serves on-ly to con-ceal a cold
in-sen-si-bil-i-ty.

Chro-nol-o-gy is an in-dis-pen sable at-tend-ant on
His-to-ry.

Hy-poc ri-sy is an as-sumed ap-pear ance of vir-tues
which the hyp o-crite does not pos-sess.

That which ap-pears to be stu-pid-i-ty in young peo-
ple is of-ten on-ly ex-ces-sive ti mid-i-ty.

En-gra-vings are made on wood, on cop-per, on steel,
and on stone. En-gra-ving on stone is called
li-thog-ra phy.

No. 126—CXXVI.

-acy=as-sy; ary=ar-ry; ory=ur-ry; ity=e-ty.

Five Syllables. Accent on Second.

con fed er a cy	ag i na ry	con sol a tor y
de gen er a cy	in cen di a ry	de clam a tor y
ef fem i na cy	o bit u a ry	de clar a tor y
in del i ca cy	pe cu ni a ry	de fam a tor y
in vet er a cy	pre lim i na ry	dis pen sa tor y
le git i ma cy	re sid u a ry	ex clam a tor y
a poth e ca ry	sub sid i a ry	in flam ma tor y
aux il i ar y	un nec es sa ry	ob serv a tor y
con tem po ra ry	vo cab u la ry	pre mon i tor y
e pis to la ry	vo lup tu a ry	pre par a tor y
ex tra or di na ry*	con fec tion er y	pro hib it or y
(tror)	com mend a tor y	re pos it or y
her ed i ta ry	con serv a tor y	sup pos i tor y

* Avoid the pronunciations *ex-tror-na-ry* and *ex-tray-ord-na-ry.*

Five Syllables. *Accent on Third.*

al i ment a ry	par lia ment' a ry
an ni·ver sa ry	(*la*)
com pli ment' a ry	sup ple ment' a ry
el e ment' a ry	tes ta ment' a ry
cor di al' i ty	in ge nu' i ty
ge ni al' i ty	per pe tu' i ty
gen er al' i ty	per spi cu' i ty
hos pi tal' i ty	su per flu' i ty
im mo ral' i ty	in cre du' li ty
im mor tal' i ty	im por tu' ni ty
in e qual' i ty	op por tu' ni ty
lib er al' i ty	im ma tu' ri ty
per son al' i ty	in se cu' ri ty
prin ci pal' i ty	per spi cac' i ty
prod i gal' i ty	per ti nac i ty
punc tu al' i ty	au then tic i ty
sen su al' i ty	ec cen tric i ty
ca pa bil' i ty	el ec tric i ty
cred i bil' i ty	mul ti plic i ty
dis a bil' i ty	rec i proc i ty
du ra bil' i ty	in si pid' i ty
fal li bil' i ty	mag na nim' i ty
flex i bil' i ty	u na nim' i ty
in a bil' i ty	in fi del' i ty
in ci vil' i ty	in sin cer' i ty
im be cil' i ty	in hu man' i ty
in do cil' i ty	con tra ri' e ty
im mo bil' i ty	no to ri' e ty
in sta bil' i ty	me di oc' ri ty
in u til' i ty	se ni or' i ty
mu ta bil' i ty	an i mos' i ty
pla ca bil' i ty	cu ri os' i ty

plau si bil' i ty
pos si bil' i ty
prob a bil' i ty
sen si bil' i ty
sol u bil' i ty
tan gi bil i ty
trac ta bil' i ty
ver sa til' i ty
vol u bil' i ty
joc u lar' i ty
pop u lar' i ty
reg u lar' i ty
sin gu lar' i ty
am bi gu' i ty
as si du' i ty
con ti gu' i ty
in con gru' i ty

gen er os' i ty
con tra dic' to ry
in tro duc' to ry
man u fac' to ry
val e dic' to ry
in ad ver' ten cy
phys i og' no my
gen e al' o gy
et y mol' o gy
ich thy ol' o gy
or ni thol' o gy
phra se ol' o gy
phys i ol' o gy
ste re og' ra phy
u ra nog' ra phy
a er os' co py
an e mos' co py

Six Syllables.   *Accent on Fourth..*

ap pli ca bil' i ty
com pat i bil' i ty
di vis i bil' i ty
im mu ta bil' i ty
im pos si bil' i ty
in sen si bil' i ty
im prob a bil' i ty
in vis i bil' i ty
prac ti ca bil' i ty
re spect a bil' i ty

re spon si bil' i ty
sus cep ti bil' i ty
con viv i al' i ty
im par ti al' i ty
po ten ti al' i ty
pu sil la nim' i ty
plen i po ten' tia ry
su pe ri or' i ty
in fe ri or' i ty
id i o syn' cra sy

Seven Syllables.   *Eight Syllables.*
Accent on Fifth.   *Accent on Sixth.*

com mu ni- ca bil' i ty
im prac ti ca bil' i ty
in com press i bil' i ty
in cor rupt i bil' i ty

in com pre hen si bil' it y
in com mu ni ca bil' i ty
un in tel lig i bil' i ty

No. 127—CXXVII.

A chair-man of a pub-lic as-sem-bly should be well versed in par-lia-ment-a-ry u-sage.

If the el-e-ment-a-ry parts of ed-u-ca-tion are im-per-fect-ly learned, it will be im-pos-si-ble to ac-quire ac-cu-rate-ly the more ad-vanced parts.

An o-bit-u-a-ry is a no-tice of a per-son's death, with a short sketch of his char-ac-ter.

A-void per-son-al-i-ties in your con-ver-sa-tion, if you do not wish to give of-fence.

Man-y dis-eas-es are he-red-i-ta-ry, that is, they de-scend from pa-rents to their chil-dren.

Ec-cen-tric-i-ty of man-ners is some-times nat-u-ral: but it may be ac-quired, and then it is more like-ly to be of-fen-sive.

Cu-ri-os-i-ty, when con-fined to prop-er ob-jects, and not car-ried to ex-cess, is wor-thy of com-men-da-tion.

Em-brace ev-er-y op-por-tu-ni-ty of do-ing good to oth-ers, and your kind-ness will be a-bun-dant-ly re-turned.

A plen-i-po-ten-tia-ry is an am-bas-sa-dor in-vest-ed with full pow-er.

The im-prac-ti-ca-bil-i-ty of at-tain-ing a wish, will pre-vent our in-dulg-ing it. No man who is in his sens-es wish-es to fly like a bird, or to swim like a fish.

Few things are more apt to of-fend than the pom-pous dis-play of su-pe-ri-or-i-ty, wheth-er re-al or im-ag-i-na-ry.

Do not seek no-to-ri-e-ty. It is sel-dom a thing to be de-sired.

The great-er your ad-van-ta-ges, the great-er are your re-spon-si-bil-i-ties.

Be not con-tent with me-di-oc-ri-ty. Aim at ex-cel-lence.

The vo-lup-tu-a-ry, from the fre-quent-ly re-peat-ed grat-i-fi-ca-tion of his ap-pe-tite, ceas-es to en-joy the pleas-ure he so ea-ger-ly pur-sues.

An ex-ces-sive sen-si-bil-i-ty some-times ex-po-ses us to un-nec-es-sa-ry pain.

The in-vet-er-a-cy of a bad hab-it is no rea-son for
yield-ing to it with-out ma-king an ef-fort to o-ver-
come it.

Pe-cu-ni-a-ry loss-es are, with man-y peo-ple, the
loss-es most sin-cere-ly la-ment-ed.

Cul-ti-vate a hab-it of punc-tu-al-i-ty. There are
oc-ca-sions up-on which the loss of a min-ute
may be the loss of a for-tune or a life.

In-fan-cy is in-tro-duc-to-ry to youth; youth is in-
tro-duc-to-ry to man-hood; man-hood is in-tro-
duc-to-ry to old age; old age is in-tro-duc-to-ry
to death; and death is in-tro-duc-to-ry to an-
oth-er and a bet-ter life.

In-cre-du-li-ty may be car-ried too far. An in-
cred-u-lous man may re-fuse to be-lieve that
which has ev-i-dence a-ble to con-vince all
oth-er men of its truth; while he re-mains in-
cred-u-lous mere-ly out of-sin-gu-lar-i-ty.

Al-a-bam-a is said to sig-ni-fy in the In-di-an
tongue, "Here we rest." The fol-low-ing is the
sto-ry of the or-i-gin of the name. A tribe of
In-di-ans were fly-ing from a re-lent-less foe in
the track-less for-est in the South-west. Wea-ry
and trav-el worn, they reached a no-ble river;
on its banks the chief of the band stuck his tent-
pole in the ground, and ex-claimed "Al-a-bam-a!
Al-a-bam-a!" which means, "Here we will rest!
Here we will rest!"

With-out as-si-du-i-ty no val-u-a-ble ac-qui-si-
tion can be made.

A val-e-dic-to-ry ad-dress is an ad-dress in which
the speak-er takes leave of his as-so-ci-ates, or
of those whom he has long served po-lit-i-cal-ly,
or whom he has com-mand-ed as a mil-i-ta-ry
of-fi-cer.

Ver-sa-til-i-ty of tal-ent is of-ten high-ly ad-van-
ta-geous to its pos-ses-sor; but there is some
dan-ger of such a per-son's be-ing led to di-
rect his at-ten-tion to too man-y sub-jects, and
there-by be-com-ing mas-ter of none.

LE.

No. 128—CXXVIII.

–cle, –kle, –dle, –fle, –gle, –ple, –tle, –zle.

Two Syllables.　Accent on First.

–cle, –kle.	dwin dle	tan gle	sta ple
cac kle	swin dle	span gle	peo ple
tac kle	bun dle	stran gle	stee ple
shac kle	trun dle	din gle	*–tle*
frec kle	hud dle	jin gle	bat tle
spec kle	pud dle	min gle	cat tle
fic kle	gir dle	sin gle	rat tle
pic kle	cur dle	an kle	tat tle
tic kle	hur dle	ran kle	prat tle
coc kle	*–fle*	sprin kle	ket tle
buc kle	baf fle	twin kle	met tle
suc kle	raf fle	gar gle	net tle
chuc kle	muf fle	*–ple*	set tle
cir cle	ruf fle	am ple	bee tle
(ser)	scuf fle	sam ple	lit tle
sur cle	shuf fle	tram ple	brit tle
cy cle	*–gle, –kle*	tem ple	bot tle
trea cle	*n=ng*	pim ple	pet tle
–dle	drag gle	sim ple	cut tle
ad dle	strag gle	rum ple	shut tle
pad dle	gig gle	crum ple	tur tle
sad dle	gog gle	pur ple	myr tle
wad dle	jug gle	ap ple	pes tle
med dle	smug gle	dap ple	*–zle, –sle, –xle*
ped dle	strug gle	grap ple	daz zle
can dle	ea gle	rip ple	driz zle
dan dle	bea gle	tip ple	noz zle
han dle	bu gle	crip ple	guz zle
nee dle	an gle	tri ple	muz zle
fid dle	dan gle	top ple	puz zle
mid dle	fan gle	sup ple	ax le
rid dle	jan gle	cou ple	mea sles
kin dle	man gle	sup ple	

.ble not preceded by a or i.

bab ble	drib ble	trou ble	jum ble
dab ble	quib ble	baw ble	rum ble
gab ble	scrib ble	fee ble	tum ble
rab ble	cob ble	no ble	crum ble
squab ble	gob ble	foi ble	mar ble
scrab ble	hob ble	gam ble	war ble
peb ble	bub ble	ram ble	trem ble
tre ble	stub ble	bram ble	sham ble
dib ble	dou ble	scram ble	thim ble

Three Syllables. Accent on first.

ar ti cle	ves i cle	sep tu ple
au ri cle	ob sta cle	oc tu ple
cur ri cle	or a cle	dec u ple
can ti cle	pin na cle	cen tu ple
chron i cle	tu ber cle	pre am ble
cu ti cle	ar bus cle	sol u ble
i ci cle	cor pus cle	vol u ble
par ti cle	car bun cle	*n=ng*
pel li cle	prin ci ple	quad ran gle
rad i cle	quad ru ple	rec tan gle
tu ni cle	quin tu ple	tri an gle
ve hi cle	sex tu ple	sur cin gle

The last four words are often heard with the accent on the second syllable.

Accent on Second.

as sem ble	en no ble	en kin dle
dis sem ble	en sam ple	en cir cle
re sem ble	ex am ple	em bez zle
en fee ble	en ti tle	in vei gle

Four and Five Syllables.

par ti ci ple	dis so lu ble	in dis so lu ble
rec ep ta cle*	res o lu ble	ir res o lu ble
per i win kle	in sol u ble	

---

* Often pronounced *re-cep'-ta-cle.*

No. 129—CXXIX.
–able and –ible.
Three Syllables. Accent on First.

af fa ble	pass a ble	for ci ble
ar a ble	pli a ble	fran gi ble
bla ma ble	port a ble	fu si ble
ca pa ble	po ta ble	hor ri ble
cul pa ble	prob a ble	leg i ble
cu ra ble	sa la ble*	man di ble
du ra ble	suit a ble	mis ci ble
ef fa ble	syl la ble	pas si ble
e qua ble	ten a ble	pos si ble
ford a ble	au di ble	plau si ble
laud a ble	cred i ble	ris i ble
li a ble	cru ci ble	sen si ble
mov a ble*	ed i ble	tan gi ble
mu ta ble	fal li ble	ter ri ble
no ta ble	fea si ble	vin ci ble
not a ble	fen ci ble	vis i ble
pal pa ble	flex i ble	ven di ble

Four Syllables. Accent on First.

ad mi ra ble	ex e cra ble	rep u ta ble
a mi a ble	ex o ra ble	rev o ca ble
am i ca ble	ex pi a ble	sea son a ble
ap pli ca ble	ex pli ca ble	sep a ra ble
cen su ra ble	fash ion a ble	ser vice a ble
com mend a ble	fa vor a ble	so ci a ble
com pa ra ble	for mid a ble	(she)

* In *movable, salable, advisable, reconcilable,* and some other words in -*able,* the *e* of the primitive is often retained, though contrary to rule, and the words are spelled *moveable, saleable, adviseable, reconcileable,* etc.

Walker retains the *e* in *moveable,* to preserve the sound of the *o;* while Webster and Worcester reject it.

com fort a ble   hab i ta ble   su per a ble
(*kum*)   hon or a ble   ter mi na ble
con· quer a ble   hos pi ta ble   trea son a ble
(*kong ker*)   ir ri ta ble   val u a ble
cred it a ble   lam en ta ble   va ri a ble
des pi ca ble   mal le a ble   veg e ta ble
dis pu ta ble   mem o ra ble   ven er a ble
du bi ta ble   mis er a ble   vio la ble
en vi a ble   nav i ga ble   vul'ner a ble
e qui ta ble   prof it a ble   dep re ca ble
(*ek kwe*) ,   rea son a ble   el i gi ble
es ti ma ble   rep a ra ble   cor ri gi ble

Four Syllables.   Accent on Second.

a do ra ble   in ef fa ble   dis cern i ble
ad vi sa ble   in flam ma ble   (*diz zern*)
a gree a ble ·   in scru ta ble   im pas si ble
al low a ble   in trac ta ble   im press i ble
ap prov a ble   ob serv a ble   in cred i ble
as sail a ble   re ceiv a ble   in del i ble
at tain a ble   re mark a ble   in fal li ble
a vail a ble   re mov a ble   in flex i ble
a void a ble   re new a ble   in fran gi ble
con ceiv a ble   re spec ta ble   in fu si ble
con form a ble   re triev a ble   in sen si ble
con so la ble   ad mis si ble   in tan gi ble
de cli na ble   com bus ti ble   in vin ci ble
de fi na ble   com press i ble   in vis i ble
de lec ta ble   con du ci ble   in ras ci ble
de mon stra ble   con temp ti ble   os ten si ble
de test a ble   cor rup ti ble   re du ci ble
ex cu sa ble   de du ci ble   re flex i ble
im pass a ble   de fen si ble   re fran gi ble
im pla ca ble   de struc ti ble   re spon si ble

Five Syllables. Accent on Second.

ap pre ci a ble
  (she)
con sid er a ble
dis cov er a ble
dis tin guish a ble
in cal cu la ble
in com par a ble
in dis pu ta ble
in du bi ta ble
in es ti ma ble
in ev i ta ble
in ex o ra ble
in ex pi a ble
in ex pli ca ble
in ex tri ca ble
in hos pi ta ble
im mem o ra ble
in im i ta ble

in nu mer a ble
in sa ti a ble
  (she)
in sep a ra ble
in suf fer a ble
in val u a ble
in va ri a ble
in vi o la ble
in vul ner a ble
ir ref ra ga ble
ir ref u ta ble
ir rep a ra ble
ir rev o ca ble
re cov er a ble
re me di a ble
re mu ner a ble
in cor rig i ble
in tel li gi ble

Five Syllables. Accent on Third.

in con so la ble
in con test a ble
in de cli na ble
in dis pen sa ble
in ex cu sa ble
in sup port a ble
in sur mount a ble
in ter change a ble
ir re claim a ble
rec on cil a ble
un a void a ble
ap pre hen si ble
com pre hen si ble

con tro vert i ble
in com pat i ble
in cor rupt i ble
in de struc ti ble
in di gest i ble
in di vis i ble
in ex haust i ble
  (egz haust)
in ex press i ble
ir re du ci ble
ir re ver si ble
rep re hen si ble

Six Syllables. –able and –ible. Accent on Third.

in com men su ra ble	in ex tin guish a ble
in com mu ni ca ble	ir re cov er a ble
in con sid er a ble	ir re me di a ble

Accent on Fourth.

ir rec on ci la ble*	in con tro vert i ble
in com pre hen si ble	ir rep re hen si ble

---

* *Irreconcilable* and *immovable* are often, perhaps generally, spelled with the *e—irreconcileable, immoveable.*

POSTSCRIPT
TO
PUBLISHER'S ADVERTISEMENT.

The volume now issued contains only the First Part and thirty-three pages of the Second Part of the complete book referred to in the "Publisher's Advertisement." The publication of this edition in advance has been rendered necessary by the demand for the "Speller and Reader," and by the slowness with which, from unavoidable causes, the work has hitherto progressed. The publisher hopes, however, to offer to the public, in a very short time, the *whole* "Speller and Reader," as prepared by the author, and still in the hands of the printer.

www.ingramcontent.com/pod-product-compliance
Lightning Source LLC
Chambersburg PA
CBHW030626270326
41927CB00007B/1327